Praise for *Your Divine Fingerprint*

"Keith Craft's *Your Divine Fingerprint* takes self-empowerment to the next level because it positively impacts your mind, heart, and spirit. Each chapter will inspire you to discover your purpose, manifest your greatness, and become an unstoppable force in pursuit of your dreams. A powerful, step-by-step guide for helping you live your greatest life."

—Les Brown, author of *Live your Dreams*

"God designed you with distinct characteristics for a unique purpose that only you can fulfill. In *Your Divine Fingerprint*, Keith Craft will help you discover, develop, and deploy leadership gifts to make a lasting difference in this world."

—Craig Groeschel, senior pastor of LifeChurch.tv

"In an approachable and humorous way, Keith Craft examines how elevating our thinking about the moments in our lives—even the horrible and uncomfortable ones—gives us momentum to become the men and women of faith and influence God created us to be. I believe *Your Divine Fingerprint* will bless anyone who reads it with the freedom to develop your own unique, God-given fingerprint."

—Robert Morris, senior pastor of Gateway Church

"This book combines information, inspiration, and practical yet profound impartation like no other book I've read. Discover your unique 'divine fingerprint' and 'your 1%' that will release the force that makes you unstoppable. Choose to make this your defining moment."

—Phil Munsey, chairman of Champions Network

"Your fingerprint leaves a mark on everything. Your fingerprint is a mark that you have been there; touched that or did this and affected something. Nothing is the same after you touch it because your mark, your fingerprint is left behind. Keith Craft shows us how our fingerprint is a unique mark of God's Divine purpose. Keith takes us inside his personal journey of success to find our 1% that is distinctive and original. I have watched Keith in various settings and engagements and personally seen his passion to help others become the unstoppable force God created. Don't just read this book: weave this book into the fabric of your life."

—Charles G. Scott, General Bishop of the
Pentecostal Church of God

Your Divine Fingerprint

Your Divine Fingerprint

The Force That Makes You Unstoppable

KEITH CRAFT

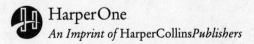

Courtesy of
Wisconsin Public Radio
wpr.org

 HarperOne

An Imprint of HarperCollins*Publishers*

HarperOne

HarperCollins books may be purchased for educational, business, or sales promotional use. For information please email the Special Markets Department at SPsales@harpercollins.com.

HarperCollins website: http://www.harpercollins.com

HarperCollins®, ♕®, and HarperOne™ are trademarks of HarperCollins Publishers.

FIRST HARPERCOLLINS PAPERBACK EDITION PUBLISHED IN 2014

Designed by Terry McGrath

Art created and used by permission of the author.

Library of Congress Cataloging-in-Publication Data

Craft, Keith.
Your divine fingerprint : the force that makes you unstoppable : / by Keith Craft.
—FIRST EDITION.
pages cm
ISBN 978–0–06–220651–0
1. Identity (Psychology)—Religious aspects—Christianity. 2. Individual differences—Religious aspects—Christianity. 3. Individuality. 4. Choice (Psychology—Religious aspects—Christianity. 5. Decision making—Religious aspects—Christianity. 6. Self-actualization (Psychology)—Religious aspects—Christianity. I. Title.
BV4509.5.C73 2013   248.4—dc23
2013019525

14 15 16 17 18 RRD(H) 10 9 8 7 6 5 4 3 2 1

I dedicate this book to my three children, who are immeasurable gifts from God to me. The fact that they all have chosen to follow Christ is a dream come true, but their choice to co-labor with me in the advancing of God's kingdom in the earth is . . . well . . . my heaven on earth!

Joshua . . . you are and always have been my Champion! On July 28, 1987, I discovered a depth of God's love I had never known as you were being born. God spoke to me and said, "Do you see what you are feeling?" Out loud, in the delivery room, I said, "Yes!" He said, "That is just what I feel about you every day." Son, my life has never been the same since that day. Every day YOU remind me how much God loves me.

Keela . . . you are my Daisy and my sunshine wrapped in one. I named you nine years before you were born. One night when your mother and I were having devotions in our sophomore year of college, I said, "We are going to have a daughter and I want to name her Keela . . . half Keith and half Sheila." You are just that baby, the BEST of your mother and me, in one gift to us and the world, from God!

Whitney . . . you are my Giggles! From the day you were born, you have brought the fragrance of God's joy to our family. I will never forget when you were six and we were driving along in the car. All of the sudden you said, "Daddy! I know what worship is!" I said, "What is it?" You said, "To be in AWE of God!" You bring me daily AWE and I am so glad the rest of the world now sees God on display through your life as a Worship Leader for Him. I so love YOU!

Your Divine Fingerprint is dedicated to my children, not just because they are my children. But they indeed are the "living epistles" of every page of this book and I am honored to say, transformational examples that the truth in this book can change your life for the better!

Contents

Your Divine Fingerprint

1

Your Defining Moments

It's not our moments that define us,
but our choices that distinguish us.

Defining moments. We all have them. What's important is not the actual moment, really. It's how we react or respond to the moment that really matters. By our own choice or not, a defining moment is an occurrence, a situation, a catastrophe, or a break-through opportunity.

Defining moments are a paradox for most people. This is because they happen all the time, and yet most of the time, we are unaware that a defining moment has happened.

Can you remember a time in your own life that was a defining moment? The kind of moment—good or bad, positive or nega-tive, healthy or unhealthy—when you allowed something about that moment to play a significant role in your life that at least to some degree has defined your existence?

When is a moment a defining moment? I believe moments are defined every time we make a decision.

The decisions you make today will not just affect your tomorrow but will determine your future.

Every day we have defining moments based on action, whether an action we have taken or an action someone else has taken in regard to us. Our decision to define the moment is what gives power to the moment. So in the end, we are the ones who determine which are the defining moments in our lives.

You may have had events in your life, your own defining moments, which challenge your very existence. No matter how old or young you are, chances are you have already faced life-challenging and life-altering situations. These moments and situations have the potential to be more than defining moments; they can be miracle moments that will shape your destiny, if you so choose. You may have:

- Experienced a catastrophic failure, personally or in your business, such as bankruptcy, a major theft, or business disruption due to fire. Maybe you were terminated.

- Experienced a huge success in your past that, when you think about it, was the best time in your life.

- Had a serious illness or accident, personally or in your immediate family. You survived the illness or accident but have physical limitations.

- Met someone who from the moment you met him, your life was forever changed for the good—or bad.

- Been badly hurt by someone whom you deeply love—or worse, you may have allowed someone who didn't love you to hurt you.

- Or you may remember a time when you made a decision that changed everything.

Today can be a new defining moment, because today you can choose to allow your past to be just what it is: past! Your past can be something you choose to help define what you want, what you don't want, how you want to be, how you don't want to be, and maybe most importantly, who you want to be and how you want to spend the rest of the best life you have now!

My Defining Moment

Friday the 13th, May of 1960.

My family lived in a suburban neighborhood of Dallas, Texas. My mother was going to a choir banquet that night, so my grandmother—Mamaw, as she was affectionately called—came to our house to babysit my brother and me.

My mom put me in a playpen next to her bed, changed her clothes, and left to enjoy the banquet. Mamaw checked on me then returned to the kitchen to clean the dishes from supper. After about a half an hour had passed, my brother came into the kitchen and said to my grandmother, "Mamaw! Mamaw! Keith's all blue!" Not knowing what my brother could possibly be talking about, Mamaw went to the bedroom where my mother had left me sleeping.

As she walked into the room, she noticed something enveloped around my body—it was a plastic laundry bag. The kind of flimsy plastic bag used by dry cleaning companies. It had contained the dress my mother wore to the banquet. Mom had changed into her dress and left the bag on the edge of the bed.

The wind from an open window had blown the bag from the bed onto me as I slept in my playpen. Mamaw could see that I had turned blue from lack of oxygen. She immediately picked me up and removed the plastic bag. Blood was flowing from my nose, ears, and mouth. I wasn't breathing.

As she held me close, Mamaw called the emergency number. She then rushed outside to wait for help to arrive. She prayed. She hoped against hope. She cried. She believed. After an excruciatingly long wait, she heard the siren, but it wasn't an ambulance she saw—instead, a fire truck. The ambulance had gotten a flat tire en route. Firemen were dispatched and arrived on the scene only to find my unconscious, lifeless body. My father, who was a Dallas policeman, received word and rushed to the scene as well. When he arrived, he saw men working furiously trying to revive me. Fireman E. R. Coffman asked for permission to use a new procedure called mouth-to-mouth resuscitation.

After several failed attempts to revive me, I was pronounced dead at the scene. It was at this moment that Mamaw prayed one last desperate prayer, "God, You are the One who gave him life and You can resurrect him!" At that moment, to everyone's astonishment, a breath of air shot out of my mouth, and my eyes popped open! I was alive! The only thing everyone knew that day was that they were all witnesses to a miracle. I was immediately transported to the hospital instead of the morgue.

There, doctors and nurses were concerned that I might have suffered severe brain damage after going without oxygen for more than a half hour. But in the hours that followed, I showed no signs of brain damage—although from time to time, I have used that experience as an excuse for any faulty brain function on my part.

Later that year, on November 24, 1960, *The Dallas Morning News* ran a cover story of the miracle. There was a picture of our entire family on the front page with the caption, "A Thanksgiving Blessing." Fireman E. R. Coffman would receive a commendation from President John F. Kennedy for the role he played in my unique miracle.

Death, at any age, could be called a defining moment. Everyone will die at some point. But it is the people who are left, whose lives are touched by the death of another, who will have to choose how the death of another defines them.

For as long as I can remember, my death-to-back-to-life experience has been a defining moment for me. I was professionally pronounced dead and super-naturally brought back to life! The doctors called it a miracle. I call it a miracle moment!

Our defining moments have miracle-working power, because it's our choice to take the good, the bad, and the ugly and turn those moments into momentums. You literally become a miracle worker when YOU choose to seize the opportunity to take whatever has happened in your life and use it for your good. My hope for you is that from this day forward, the only thing that will define you are the moments you have used to create momentum for miracles.

Moments into Miracles

My 1828 Webster's dictionary defines *miracle* as "a wonderful thing; an event or effect contrary to the established construction and cause of things; a supernatural event."

Not all moments are wonderful things, but every moment can be a super-natural event, because regardless of the construction of a moment, or the cause of a thing, every person has the power to choose how a moment is defined. We cannot determine everything that happens to us, but we can define how what happens affects us.

So, how does a moment become a miracle? There is something inside you that gives you this power! I will talk about it later in this book. In fact, it is what this book is all about. I call it the 1% Factor. It is not only the thing that makes you different than everyone who has ever been born or will be born, but it is also the revelation of this uniqueness that will empower you to become a miracle worker!

Miracles don't just happen, but moments do. When we take natural moments, negative or positive, and use them to create positive momentum, the moment becomes a super-natural moment—a miracle! When we choose to see the positive in the negative, we are creating momentum in the moment. When we choose to learn from our experiences both good and bad, we are creating momentum, because we are choosing to grow. When you choose to be an Energy Producer and not an Energy Demander (more about this later in the book), you create momentum in any moment. When you understand that your attitude is the hinge that the door of your destiny swings on, you create momentum in any moment to open any door!

When we understand the power we have to choose how a moment will affect us, we can then begin to define the moment instead of the moment defining us. It's at that point that moment + momentum = miracle. You have the power to turn moments into miracles. Rather than having defining moments, we have miracle moments that define a super-natural life, and we can overcome all natural limitations and deficiencies.

How many miracles have occurred in your life, recognized or otherwise? Maybe you haven't seen your moments as miracles. But the truth is, to some degree, you have overcome incredible challenges to be where you are in life today. Whether you recognize God or not, Friday, May 13, 1960, wasn't just a defining moment—it was a miracle moment. Everyone there that day witnessed more than a moment—they witnessed a miracle moment.

There is miracle-working power in moments that we use to define us. Regardless of the physical, emotional, financial, or mental outcome, we choose just how much power a moment has over us. We can permit ourselves to be defined by that label, or we can choose to recognize the experience as just that: an experience that we use to move forward into our future.

Not all defining moments are bad situations or experiences. A defining moment may be a moment that takes your breath away. I refer to this quote frequently: "Life is not measured by the number of breaths you take but by the moments that take your breath away." The author is unknown. Unfortunately for most of us, the only time we allow something to take our breath away is in tragedy. I encourage you, today, to make a choice, to allow good moments, good times, and good people to take your breath away.

We all have unique stories and unique experiences. But our stories and our experiences are not what make us unique. It is WHO YOU ARE that makes you unique.

Unique means "radically distinctive and without equal; being the only one of its kind."

What makes you unique? Is it a defining moment, or who you are at your core level?

The answer to that question is the purpose of this book. It is your 1% Factor that gives you the ability to defy the odds. You are an odds defier. You started life with the odds against you as a sperm swimming upstream with five million other sperm. There was only one egg. The odds were 5,000,000:1. You made it! You were radically distinctive and without equal. You were not just the only one of your kind—YOU were the only one! The odds will never be stacked against you like that again. Your 1% Factor began that day.

Then, you were born. Did you know it is believed that when you are born, it is the closest you will ever come to dying without dying? You have exceeded the odds, going from a sperm to being born with a unique fingerprint that makes YOU an Unstoppable Force! You achieved what 4,999,999 other sperm couldn't do! Regardless of what has happened in your life since that time, you are unique. You defied the worst possible odds to be here, and if any moment thus far can define you, that's it! You are a miracle and if you are a miracle, YOU can be a MIRACLE WORKER! You have a 1% Factor no other person has on earth.

Take the Challenge

My desire is for this book to challenge you. It is about choices that you can make that will turn your moments into miracles. First, I want to challenge you to believe BIGGER than maybe you ever have. I want to challenge you to believe not only that God created you but also that God loves you and has a great purpose for your life.

There is a scripture in the Bible, John 3:16 (MSG), that tells us how much God loves us. It is probably the most familiar verse in the world: "This is how much God loved the world: He gave His Son, His one and only Son. And this is why: so that no one need be destroyed; by believing in Him, anyone can have a whole and lasting life."

When I think about someone who turned a moment into a miracle, I have to think of who I believe is the greatest leader who has ever lived, Jesus. In what was the worst moment in Jesus's life, He used death to give us life. The moment Jesus died on the cross, He chose to create not only momentum for our miracle of a super-natural life but momentum as well for His own miracle: His resurrection! If He had not died, there would have been no resurrection. No death, no life.

The moment of the cross does not define Jesus. The moments of pain and suffering do not define Jesus. Jesus took the bad moments, the difficult moments, the painful moments, and because of His choice to die on the cross, He turned those moments into momentum to produce miracle-working power. Jesus is not defined by being a man who suffered, or by all the horrible things that He endured. He is not defined as a man who died on a cross. He is defined by the miracle moment of His resurrection. He is defined by the miracle-working power He has because of the miracle moments He made through His choices.

This book is about your choices. This book is a journey about how YOU can Discover, Develop, and Deploy your 1%. Your 1% is the super-natural part of you that has the power to take any moment in your life—past, present, or future—and turn it into momentum. It's about taking those moments that would normally define you because of what happened, and using them to create momentum that produces your miracle-filled life.

I want to encourage you to be intentional about living a life of greater purpose. I hope to show you how to Discover, Develop, and Deploy your 1% Factor. I can't wait for you to discover how unique you are, that you have a purpose no one else on earth has ever had. My desire is for you to learn something about yourself that perhaps you have never known and to realize that you have greatness in you that others need.

> *You have a unique fingerprint that no one else has, to leave a unique imprint that no one else can leave.*

The 1% Adventure Begins

I am going to take you on an adventure that I believe could change your life forever. I will show you how thinking differently about yourself, your moments, your life, and your future will produce an outcome you never thought possible. We will explore together how small adjustments in a thought process can impact an outcome. I will share how to establish and live a core values–based life, a worthy and desirable trait of a purposeful life.

Most importantly, I will share my process and strategies for discovering, developing, and deploying your greatness, what I call your 1%. My process and strategies are proven. They work. They will work for you.

This is the beginning of a new paradigm for you, one that will prove to you that you have greatness, you are unique, and you have a special purpose to fulfill.

The THINK, BE, DO Triad of Discover, Develop, and Deploy That Leads to HAVE

As the diagram displays, I utilize a triad-based system in my life. I train executives, corporations, and nonprofit organizations on how to implement this system as a process and strategy for greater growth and efficiency, increased profitability, and improved overall operations. It will scale for individuals, small to mid-size business, large corporations, and even governments. It is guaranteed to work for you too.

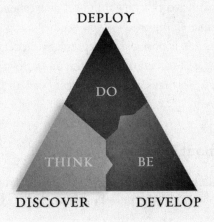

DEPLOY

DO

THINK   BE

DISCOVER   DEVELOP

I will cover my triad process in more depth in Chapter 4, "Your Think, Be, Do." I introduce the triad system here as a reference because I want you to see it, believe it, and be confident that I am not going to take you blindly down an unfamiliar road. I will share with you from the beginning my process and strategy that leads to successful, purposeful living.

You will discover what your journey can be when you discover that who you choose to be is more important than who you have been. Your 1% Factor is indeed your X Factor for Success!

As you get to know me, you will realize I am a person who genuinely cares about you, your today, your tomorrow, and your future. I don't hold back. The God I serve gave His best for me. I will give my best for you. My passion is to walk in excellence, to be my best. Not just sometimes or when I feel like it, but to give my best in everything I do. I have made a choice to be this way. It is my highest and best use. When I bring my best—give my best with excellence—others benefit. And I do too. At this stage of growth, choosing to adopt a new paradigm or not, it is reasonable to expect internal struggles. Should I or shouldn't I? Let me encourage you . . . you should. Move beyond the idea of what I call normalcy and accept a new mind-set of excellence. Perfection isn't possible. Being the best you can be, doing the best you can do all the time, is possible. Once I made the decision to simply be the best I can all the time, the pressure to perform was off. No excuses. No stress. Just be the best I can all the time.

A Word About Mamaw

A lot of thought went into naming this chapter "Your Defining Moments." It was God who raised me from the dead; it was God who saved me from brain damage. But it was Mamaw who deployed her 1%. Her 1% Factor helped to create my miracle moment. Mamaw became my hero, my mentor and role model in life. Not because she prayed me back to life but because of the odds she defied to Discover, Develop, and Deploy her 1%.

By May 13, 1960, Mamaw had experienced a life-shattering divorce. After being diagnosed with breast cancer, her husband left her. She went on to have a double mastectomy. The mastectomy wasn't the worst part; the radiation used to kill the cancer was. Her entire upper body was burned, and she lived the rest of her life with serious physical complications, including open wounds that would not heal.

Mamaw was not defined by the divorce. She was not defined by the horror of cancer. She was not defined by the plague of her daily pain and suffering. She was defined by the same thing that this book will teach you to use to define yourself: the 1% Factor. Mamaw's fingerprint has made an indelible imprint on my life and has fueled the passion in me to do the same for others.

It was God who has given me countless miracles in my life. And it is God who can and will do the same thing for you!

In the next chapter, I will begin to unfold the marvel I have labeled the X Factor. But before we go there, I challenge you to discover specifics of your life as you begin to explore the THINK, BE, DO process. Take all the time you need to be thorough.

There is more that defines you than meets the eye. The 1% Factor will help you Discover, Develop, and Deploy your uniqueness; achieve the highest levels of success; and live an elevated life.

THINK, BE, DO

THINK: Discover

What is your defining moment that created the momentum for your miracle moment? Write down in detail the miracle moment that has shaped who you are today.

What talent, skill, or passion drives you? Make a list of your talents, skills, and passions that drive you, that you enjoy, that other people recognize in you.

What is truly unique about you? Write down everything that you believe you do better than anyone else you know.

BE: Develop

Based on your miracle moment shaping your life, what one outcome drives your passion most? Why?

How can you develop your talent, skill, or passion into a greater part of your life?

DO: Deploy

Take the first step toward your plan.

Find a mentor to guide and encourage you.

As you read this book, BELIEVE! Believe you are special! Believe you have Greatness! Believe God has a plan for your life and that you have been given the fingerprint you have for a reason. Believe you have incredible God-given value to bring everywhere you go, and begin bringing it NOW!

2

Your X Factor
for Success

*You can't change your past,
but you can change your future.*

Most people never know they have an X Factor. They define
themselves by ethnicity or the era of history in which they
were born. They define themselves by the place they are from,
whether they're rich or poor, their nationality, their previous
successes or failures, the color of their eyes or hair, or any
number of other personal distinctions.

Misconception Leads to Preconception

All of us can get lost in the sea of humanity and just think that
we are who and what other people say we are based on their
preconceptions. All of us have preconceptions about other
people. We preconceive about people based on how we perceive
ourselves. In other words, we don't see people, places, and things

how they are—we see them through the lens of how we are. For example, if you look at a lemon with sunglasses that have blue lenses, what color is the lemon? Green . . . right? No, it is yellow. The color of the lemon does not change, but how we see the lemon does.

Most people's preconceptions stem from the misconceptions they have about themselves, based on what they have come to believe about themselves. We all have limited knowledge about ourselves. According to *Scientific American*, it is a myth that we only use 10 percent of our brain power. Neurologist Barry Gordon at Johns Hopkins School of Medicine says the "10 percent myth" is completely false.

Exposing the "10 Percent Myth"

From psychologist William James, who said, "We are making use of only a small part of our possible mental and physical resources," to Albert Einstein, who perpetuated the myth, our limited knowledge has caused misconceptions that have led to limited preconceptions. Gordon goes on to say "the 10 percent myth" about our brains comes from people's own feelings that, mentally speaking, they are coming up short because they are not tapping fully into the power of their brains. This is a misconception of our own brain capacity and impacts not only how we preconceive others but also how we misconceive them. "It turns out though, that we use virtually every part of the brain, and that [most of] the brain is active almost all the time." Ultimately, it's not that we use 10 percent of our brains but merely that we understand how only about 10 percent of it functions.[1]

YOU were created to be UNSTOPPABLE! I believe God created us in His image and likeness (Gen. 1:26). That means to

Think, Be, and Do (we will discuss this in Chapter 4 in detail) the way God does things and with the same power He does them! But limited knowledge has led to misconceptions about ourselves and has limited our perception about everything and everyone. So we live naturally rather than super-naturally, limited by our knowledge that forms our beliefs that birth our opinions. The worst part of this is that we not only STOP ourselves, but we also stop others' influence in our lives. We live too much life with presets from our family of origin and our limited knowledge about who we really are and why we are who we are. Think about it—we only know what we know, and what we don't know about ourselves can in fact hurt us.

Limited Knowledge Can Kill YOU

One of my mentors and historic shapers of my Think, Be, Do in life is the famed Russell Conwell, the founder of Temple University. He was solely responsible for raising the initial seven million dollars that were needed to build Temple University. He accomplished this by speaking more than six thousand times across the country, telling the now-famous story, "Acres of Diamonds."[2]

It was a true story about a Persian farmer named Ali Hafed, who owned a vast piece of property and one day heard about other farmers who had made millions by discovering diamond mines. This so excited the farmer that he could not wait to sell his farm and search for diamonds himself.

So he sold his farm and spent the rest of his life searching the world for the valuable gems that brought such high prices around the world. After years of endlessly searching, he ran out of money and became despondent. Finally, broken, left with nothing and no hope for the future, he jumped to his death from the coast of Barcelona, Spain, and drowned.

Meanwhile, the man who had bought his farm noticed one day a large beautiful stone in a stream that ran through the property. It was the first of many diamonds discovered there. In fact, what was once Ali Hafed's farm became the diamond mine of Golconda, one of the most magnificent diamond mines in all of history. The Kohinoor and the Orloff of the crown jewels of England and Russia, the largest on earth, came from that mine.

Limited knowledge leads to misconceptions. Ali Hafed didn't know he already had diamonds, so he went seeking them elsewhere. Misconceptions determine our preconceptions that keep us from achieving success on the level we could because we don't have the knowledge of how special, unique, and wonderful we really are. This is what makes your 1% so important. As you discover that there is a 1% difference in you and every individual, your 1%—your X Factor—not only differentiates you from others but also begins to catapult the best part of you into every part of your life!

The term *X Factor* is currently used and has been used in the past to promote products, make exorbitant claims about a product's ability to produce results, and in all types of sales and marketing literature for years. The term isn't new. The application of the term *X Factor* may in fact be overused; as in many aspects, it is to blame for under-delivering. I think all of us would agree that throughout history, there have been products that have been overpromised that under-deliver. From antiaging drugs, vitamins, diet pills, to any supposed breakthrough product that has ever hit the market, it's easy to believe that there is no real X Factor for anything.

In spite of this, I find the term not just appropriate but also powerful when it comes to you and me. I can use the term *X Factor* because each one of us really does have it! We just need to discover what it is. Until I realized that I had an X Factor, I did not see myself as having any distinctive greatness. And if we can't see greatness in ourselves, how could we ever see it or benefit from the greatness in others?

All personal greatness lies beyond the normal self. The desire to be the best you that you can be—along with daily disciplines and long-term commitment—will awaken potential greatness and produce GREATNESS results.

X Factor Defined

X Factor is defined as "the element or elements that are vital to an observable change or result." In other words, all things being equal, if you just add X to an equation, process, or strategy, X will produce a result that cannot be produced in any other way. Stated yet another way, without X in the mix, a desired result will not occur.

People have searched far and wide for the X Factor that will make them succeed in a way that nothing else can, and yet the answer is not just within reach, it's within YOU! There is a very important question that you must answer before we can move forward: What do you want?

> *Most people get more of what they don't*
> *want rather than what they do want because*
> *they never decide what it is they want.*

My point is simple. People want to succeed but have not taken the time to define success. Success defined by the movies—fast cars, attractive companions, pockets full of cash, and mansions on the hillside—is great, but is that what we really want? One of the great influencers in my life was Zig Ziglar. I often heard Zig say, "Most people climb the ladder of success and when they get to the top, they realize that the ladder is leaning against the wrong wall." I am not saying having things is bad; I am saying you must define what success is for you. Many people put unrealistic pressure on themselves to have material things without attempting to define exactly what success means in their life.

My desire is to present what I believe to be the X Factor required for you to live an elevated life of maximum achievable success FOR YOU. Most people will accept this as maximum productivity, highest effectiveness, and personal significance. *The Elevated Life* is another book.

The X Factor for your success is your 1%! But again, most people haven't even known they had a 1% that is their X Factor for Success! Without first Discovering and Developing this 1%, it is impossible to Deploy their X Factor!

Keep reading! You're about to discover just how AWESOME you are and that you have been "fearfully and wonderfully made!" as the Bible says in Psalms 139:14 (NIV).

All throughout this book, we will look at your 1% through the lens of the Think, Be, Do triad. The most important thing you need to know is how to Discover, Develop, and Deploy your 1%.

The redundancy is ON PURPOSE because I want you to get it! As Dr. Phil McGraw says, "You either get it or you don't." I want to encourage you to be THE person who GETS your 1% so the world can GET the BEST of YOU! Let's look at the triad from Chapter 1 again.

> **THINK:** DISCOVER—Discover the 1% that makes you unique.
>
> **BE:** DEVELOP—Develop your gifts, talents, competencies, visions, and passions.
>
> **DO:** DEPLOY—Deploy your 1% Factor to take your life to the next level of success that you desire and that you have been created to achieve.

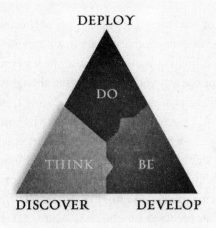

My triad process will be explained more in-depth in Chapter 4. I have included it here as a reference and to visually express how you will use your 1% for greater results. My proven process is strategically based on one primary triad, the THINK, BE, DO triad. The systematic process always starts at THINK. I have proven that if people will simply change their thinking, they will change their lives.

But change isn't always positive, and change isn't always challenging. If I change something, it doesn't always mean it's for the better. I have carefully chosen to use the term *elevate*. *To elevate* is "to lift up or make higher." Elevate is always about making something better.

Elevate your thinking. Elevate your life.

Discover

One percent of your life is completely distinctive and original, and it is a 1% uniqueness that occurs in all dimensions and aspects of your life. For example, look at the way you think, the way you act, or the way you form your first thoughts and impressions about situations.

In this book, I hope to help you discover who you are, why you are how you are, why you are sometimes a particular way versus another way, and how you can begin to shape the future you want. This will happen as you begin to apply the process of Discovering what makes you unique. As you THINK, BE, DO in all areas of your life, your uniqueness—your 1% Factor—will become clear.

I want to encourage you to journal in the process. Revelation seldom appears when you have time for it. Waiting until later to record a momentary thought or new revelation will allow the specific details to blur with time, even to the point of slipping away from you. Revelation appears at times of activity, in the course of action. Maintaining a journal helps you track and identify the thought process so you can DISCOVER, DEVELOP, and DEPLOY your 1% uniqueness.

It is critical for you to acknowledge and accept that you have 1% uniqueness. Unless and until you are willing to accept and acknowledge that you are truly unique, you will not be able to recognize your true greatness, or the greatness in others. And until you are willing to discover your own unique purpose on this earth, you will not develop it with your whole heart, mind, soul, and strength.

Some people get hung up on the thought of having greatness. But being unique also means you have value—therefore, you have a degree of greatness. The more you recognize your value, the more you should understand your unique greatness. We can understand the importance of how value reveals our greatness by answering this question: What value do I bring to anything I value? The more value you bring to your job, the greater your role in that job. The greater your role, the more valuable you are. The more value you bring to a relationship, the greater the relationship will be. So in the end, value breeds greatness, and greatness breeds value! Your greatness is your X Factor—it's your 1%! What sets you apart is the greatness you possess, which makes you more valuable to everyone and with everything you are a part of!

Develop

For your uniqueness, the Discover process alone isn't enough. Developing your 1% is not an additive, cumulative process. It is a multiplying, catapulting process. Development requires desire, determination, and dedication. Your gifts are just that—your gifts. Only you can develop the gifts you have been given. You're not gifted in everything, but you're gifted in something. But only you can Discover and Develop your Gifts.

Your Gifts and Talents

An important Gifts question: What am I truly gifted at? For instance, you may be gifted athletically, but you have to develop those gifts into talents. I can play most sports relatively well. I went to college on a basketball scholarship and was even recruited by the Dallas Cowboys to play football many years ago. But just because I am a gifted athlete doesn't mean I can play all sports well. Golf, for me, is the great equalizer. I can do it, but I am taking lessons to become a talented golfer. Your Talents are what will bring you joy professionally and recreationally.

An important Talents question: What natural Talents do I have that will help me enjoy my life, and that maybe can help others to do the same? The word *talent* originates from the Greek word *talanton*, which denotes "balance, weight, or sum of money." It was originally used in the context of money, and the more talanton you had, the more the balance and scales of life weighed in your favor. In Matthew 25, we learn that talents were given according to a person's unique ability to handle talents. So a gift, or talent, is something of notable capacity that is a characteristic feature, aptitude, or endowment a person has.

You may say, "I really don't think I am gifted or talented, and if I am, I don't know in what." Well, let me show you that you are gifted and talented. Your 1% depends on you knowing that.

You know you are gifted and talented when:

- What you do comes naturally to you
- You really enjoy what you do
- Time is never an issue
- You feel fulfilled when you do what you do

- You excel at what you do
- You want to learn more about it
- You feel like you were made to do it
- What you do is in your strength zone

In *Now, Discover Your Strengths,* Marcus Buckingham and Donald O. Clifton state that most people do not use their strengths, which thus lie dormant. Your talents are gifts from God that, when developed, show the world a part of God that has never been displayed before.

Conversely, you know you are not gifted and talented in an area if what you do brings no joy, it's hard for you to do, and you are miserable doing it. Your 1% Factor becomes Your Unstoppable Force when you begin to really Discover, Develop, and Deploy your gifts and talents to the fullest.

Your Competencies

Your Competencies are based on what you are gifted and talented in but are different from Talents. I have to continually develop my competencies based on what I want and what I want to do. My competencies are an outgrowth of my gifts and talents, but my X Factor to do the best I possibly can is up to me. My competencies are the external proof of the talents and gifts I have developed.

An important Competency question is: What Competencies do I need to develop to become better at what I want to do and will help me function in my best and highest use?

Your Vision

Your Vision is your picture of the future you want. Vision drives Passion. In fact, if you are ever in a situation, like marriage, and you find you have lost your Passion, go back to the Vision you originally had for your marriage. Your Vision is . . . your Vision. What you see is what you will get! When you Develop your Vision and Passion, you can begin to understand what it means to be UNSTOPPABLE!

An important Vision question: What do I see in my future?

An important Passion question: What energy am I willing to put forth for what I want?

Most of all, successful development is a process that influences a person to take aim. It puts one's uniqueness on a course toward achievement.

Deploy

Third, the Deployment of your 1% is subject to four main forces: your capacity to develop yourself, your ability to dream, your ability to believe, and your willingness to take action.

Your Capacity to Develop Yourself

Your Capacity to develop yourself will determine what is Deployed in your life. Have you ever thought about your personal capacity? One of the definitions of *capacity* is "the maximum amount that something can contain." It's the ability to receive knowledge. But another side of capacity is the ability to perform or produce at one's maximum! I believe that what's inside you will determine what comes out of you. Capacity is a two-way street.

Your Ability to Dream

I've never met a person who set her sights on becoming a failure. I've never heard anyone say, "I want to fail." Just the opposite! Every person I've ever met seems to have a built-in intuition that life can and should be something more than what it currently is. This innate intuition or perception that there is something greater out there somewhere is at the basis of all religions. It is at the foundation of all aspirations, inventions, innovations, and truly noble accomplishments. It is the ability to dream big dreams with all expectation for accomplishment.

It is human nature to want to take life to a higher level. For some people who live in circumstances that are physically and/or psychologically harsh, the ability to dream may be extinguished at an early age. Of course, we have all heard about people who refuse to give up on their dreams despite the worst circumstances. Two such examples are Henry Ford and Ted Geisel.

Henry Ford was the son of a farmer, but he had a dream. After his mother passed away when he was twelve, Henry was expected to take over the family farm. But Henry had a dream. He had a passion for machines that could ease the lives of farmers and replace work animals with machines. When he was seventeen, he left for Detroit to pursue his dream. By the time he was thirty-two, he completed his first horseless carriage called the Quadricycle. Two different times, Ford joined investors to establish a company that would manufacture automobiles. Neither Detroit Automobile Company nor Henry Ford Company made it more than a year. On his third attempt, the Ford Motor Company sold its first car on July 15, 1903. The rest is history.

Ted Geisel grew up in Springfield, Massachusetts. There was nothing seemingly special or unique about Ted. As a child he worked in his father's brewery, but his life began to change when his father was appointed to the Springfield Park Board. It was at the Springfield Zoo that Geisel began to Discover, Develop, and Deploy his X Factor for Success. Every day he would bring his sketch pad and pencil to draw exaggerated images of the animals.

After graduating from Dartmouth College in 1925 with a liberal arts degree, Ted went on to Lincoln College in Oxford to study English literature. A classmate, Helen Palmer, noticed his crazy fascination with drawing weird-looking animals. She convinced him to leave school after only a year and pursue his passion: drawing weird-looking beasts! Upon returning to the United States, Ted married Helen and took a job freelancing cartoons for *The Saturday Evening Post*. By 1936, he had begun to write illustrated children's books, and by 1937, had been rejected by twenty-seven publishers.

On the way home from his twenty-seventh rejection and ready to burn his manuscript, Geisel ran into an old college buddy who was now editor of children's books with Vanguard Press. Mike McClintock liked the book and decided to publish *And to Think that I Saw It on Mulberry Street*. Dr. Seuss went on to publish forty-six children's books, receive seven honorary doctorates, and win the 1984 Pulitzer Prize. His books have become classics, and his characters now appear in movies, on merchandise, and in theme parks.

His last book, *Oh, the Places You'll Go!*, speaks to every person who will go on the 1% journey.

Nothing happens without a dream.
For something really great to happen,
it takes a really great dream.

Your Ability to Believe

The common thread in these success stories is that these men discovered their 1%, developed it to its utmost potential, and deployed it with excellence. They believed! They took action to achieve the desired outcome. Every person who makes a great dream come true will face what seem to be insurmountable obstacles. Henry Ford had reasons to go back to the farm. Dr. Seuss had twenty-seven reasons to give up! But they both kept on believing. They kept on taking action toward their dreams.

Why don't all dreams come true? Could it be that we have a limited knowledge about what we are capable of? Could it be that each of us has an X Factor and that we don't know the awesome capacity we have? YOU have greatness in you to do GREAT things! I believe that to be the real truth!

Your Willingness to Take Action

I know I have had thoughts like, *What is the difference between that person and me? What have they discovered that I don't know?* Honestly, I have thought at times that I was not as gifted or talented as others were. I have also had thoughts like, *Maybe if I could just get close to their greatness, it would rub off on me!* or *How can I meet the right people?* I have had thoughts like, *If I just had more money, I could make my dreams happen.*

The bottom line is this: some people don't know how to take action to take their life to the next level. Fear of failure, fear of success, fear of change, and complacency, insecurity, lack of commitment, not knowing what they really want—or, most importantly, not knowing WHO they really are—these are very real kill factors that keep our X Factor from being known. In other cases, the failure is due to a lack of belief in oneself, and therefore a lack of action.

What would have happened if:

- Thomas Edison had listened to teachers who said he was too stupid to learn anything? He would not hold the world record for patents (1,093), including the light bulb, phonograph, film projector, and motion pictures, or have founded General Electric, one of the most successful companies in American history.

- Winston Churchill, who failed the sixth grade, believed he was a failure? He would never have become prime minister of England and been considered one of the greatest leaders in the history of the world.

- Walt Disney, who went bankrupt, had just quit? He went on to create eighty-one feature films and receive 950 honors, including forty-eight Academy Awards. He founded the California Institute of the Arts and . . . built Disneyland!

The Power of YOUR Belief

What you believe is more important than what anyone will ever tell you. What you believe about life, relationships, money, food, love, sex, exercise, food, pets, God, politics, business, heaven and hell, the economy, and last but not least, YOURSELF will drive all your behaviors and the actions you take.

Our beliefs are like the roots of a tree—the deeper they go, the higher the tree potentially grows. If I were to ask you, "What is the most important part of a tree?" I hope your answer would be, "The roots!" It is an indisputable fact. Your beliefs are like the roots of a tree, and they become the cause for success or failure in your life.

The roots of a tree are like your Belief System:

- You cannot see them, but they determine what you do see.

- How deep the roots go determine how high the tree grows.

- The roots never stop growing.

My personal belief is that it is our job to believe, and it is God's job to do the impossible. However, as powerful as our beliefs are, belief alone is not enough. We must do something with our belief. The gap between our belief and God doing the impossible is . . . our taking action. It is our responsibility to act on what we believe.

I believe there are many people who give up on their dreams way too soon because they allow kill factors to destroy their X Factor. I want to encourage you, from this point on, not to give yourself an excuse for failure. I want to lovingly challenge you to do what is required to Discover, Develop, and Deploy YOUR 1%. Take action on what you read in the pages of this book. Dare to believe that it works, and I believe you will succeed like never before.

A failure to believe always results in a failure to take action. A failure to take action results in a failure to achieve.

The Goal Is Success

What determines a person's awareness of her 1%? Definitely, the way she thinks. It is that person's thought process—her understanding and her working definition of the word *success*. *Success* is defined as (1) "the attainment of wealth, possessions, fame, or honors"; (2) "achieving a satisfactory performance"; and (3) "a favorable or prosperous termination of endeavors."

Everybody I know wants to be successful—or more successful. When I ask people what they mean by success, I usually get a wide variety of answers. Some see success strictly in financial or materialistic terms. Some see success in family terms, while others see success in spiritual terms. Still others see it in terms of their career potential or their current job situation.

Not only do the definitions differ, but the degrees of success also differ. To some, success is having enough money to pay monthly bills. To others, it is having a financial investment portfolio that allows a person or family to live well on the interest produced. To others, it is the ability to inspire tremendous contributions toward projects that can change nations.

To some, success is the ability to conceive a child. To others, it is the ability to keep a marriage together over a lifetime. To others, it is to build a family dynasty that will have an impact on society.

To some, success is having peace in one's heart, or maximizing the percentage of time one feels happy. To some, success is having a personal relationship with God. To others, it's winning the world for God.

My definition of success:
Success is an ongoing process of Discovering your
unique 1%, Developing your gifts, and Deploying
your best for the best interest of others.

Success is relative to your position in life. If you are in a negative situation in life, then success is transitioning into a more positive situation. If you have set specific goals involving change, success is accomplishing your goals. If you are facing a problem, success is solving that problem in a way that brings maximum benefit.

Success is positive and measurable. It can produce motivation. It is contagious. Varying levels of success infuse confidence and build endurance. But remember, success is an ongoing process. Maybe you are going through a rough time right now. How do you measure success in rough times? I believe that if you grow through what you go through, you will create a BREAK-THROUGH! So at times, let's measure our growth in our attitude. Let's measure our growth in our relationships. Let's identify in tough times what we need to learn. That will make a negative experience work for us rather than against us. Can failure be part of a success journey? Absolutely! Countless people have failed multiple times before achieving incredible success. They used each of those failures as a learning experience. In your tough times, remember the stories about Henry Ford, Dr. Seuss, Thomas Edison, and Walt Disney! Never let what you consider to be failure define you. Define your moments and you will create momentum for your future miracle!

As you discover your 1%, it will influence your THINKING about success. Your uniqueness elevates your views of success. For all of us, there is what has been—the Past. There is what is—the Present. And there is what is possible—the Future! Success is not a state of being—it is an ongoing process. As such, success requires ongoing effort, ongoing self-leadership, and ongoing appreciation and gratitude for both past and present accomplishments.

Your X Factor is your key to success. Your 1% uniqueness Discovered, Developed, and Deployed gives YOU the capacity to be an Unstoppable Force.

I am excited we are on this journey together! In the next chapter, we talk about your 1%. Get ready . . . your life is about to change for the better—forever!

THINK, BE, DO

THINK: Discover

How do you define *success?*

What do you consider to be the X Factor that produces success in your life?

What is your big dream?

BE: Develop

What are the next important steps ahead of you to elevate your success?

How can your 1% be applied to take you to the next level?

What is the next step to living your dream?

DO: Deploy

You have identified steps to elevate your success. Implement those steps.

Apply one idea to move you forward to your next level.

Take an action step forward to living your dream.

3

Your 1%

Your 1% difference is a deposit of
God's glory that makes you great!

My father, James Craft, was a Dallas policeman. During the early 1960s, he was a patrolman promoted to acting detective to work in fingerprinting. He was actually in the Texas School Book Depository building right after the JFK assassination. Throughout his career, he encountered criminals who attempted to sand off their fingerprints using a wide variety of mechanical and chemical means. Their attempts never worked, and generally speaking, their attempts often produced various mutilations of their skin. The irony in trying to remove fingerprints is that the person mutilating their own flesh actually creates a new identifiable pattern of mutilation print!

Fingerprint Power

Fingerprints have an almost uncanny ability to remain and regenerate.

My dad has taught me many great things that have proven invaluable in my life. For one, no two fingerprints are exactly alike. The difference may be minuscule, even less than a 1 percent difference, but the difference exists and can be used to identify a person at any point in his lifetime.

Other interesting facts about fingerprints I learned were:

- Fingerprints begin to appear when we are only three months old.

- Fingerprints are one of the last things to disappear after death.

Fingerprinting remains the most commonly gathered forensic evidence worldwide, and in most jurisdictions, fingerprint examination outnumbers all other forensic examination case-work combined.

It is very interesting to me that the only reference most of us think about when it comes to a fingerprint is how someone's fingerprint can be used to identify them related to a crime. One of the primary purposes I have written this book is because I want you to know that your 1% is evidenced in your Divine Fingerprint!

In years past, people's fingerprints were a primary identifier of people involved in crimes and accidents, whether they were victims or culprits. A person's fingerprints and dental records (bite mark) are identifiers of that person as a unique individual. With recent advancements in human genome mapping, the use of DNA as an identifier has further strengthened the significance of an individual's fingerprint power in identifying his uniqueness.

Scientists and forensic experts are on record confirming each person is unique based solely on fingerprints. Dental records and even the iris of a person's eye confirm uniqueness in individuals, as do footprints. Furthering this thought, DNA has gone above and beyond fingerprints, bite marks, and the iris to confirm individuality in people.

But not only do these elements confirm your uniqueness, the human genome mapping process also proves that people world-wide are essentially 99% alike! If all people on earth are 99% the same, and DNA, fingerprints, bite marks, and irises can prove individuality, then regardless of how you do the math, you are unique!

And since you are unique, and since you are part of the total population, there has to be a reason for your uniqueness. You bring something to the population no one else brings. You literally have Fingerprint Power! You have power at your finger-tips! Your unique fingerprint is what will give you the power to leave an imprint on people, places, and things that you come into contact with. God gave you your fingerprint so you could exem-plify GREATNESS!

Your Amazing DNA

When a man and a woman come together to have a child, there are over 8,600,000 possibilities for their child! From hair color to body shape and blood type. Who we are as individuals seems limitless. Human beings are all similar in design. We have the same cellular and tissue functions, number and location of muscles and bones, internal organs, and the ability to taste, smell, touch, see, and hear.

Without going into a biology lesson on DNA, allow me to provide some basic insight. DNA stands for deoxyribonucleic acid. It is a nucleic acid that contains the genetic instructions used in the development and functioning of all known living organisms. DNA is basically the manual used inside the human body that provides instruction at the cellular level. An amazing thing about this instruction manual is it provides all the instructions to each cell in your body for proper functioning without you having to think a single thought about it. It is totally automatic!

Here are some interesting DNA facts:

- Our bodies are composed of trillions of cells. One trillion as a number looks like this: 1,000,000,000,000.

- Each cell contains forty-six chromosomes. If cells were enlarged to the size of an aspirin pill, our DNA would be 109 football fields long.

- Each chromosome has two molecules of DNA. The DNA is composed of three billion subunits—the chemical bases A, T, C, and G.

- The order and sequence of the subunits form genetic words, and the words form genetic sentences. These sentences are called genes and contain the instructions or blueprints for proteins that perform all life functions.

- If you pulled out the DNA from a single human cell and stretched it out, it would be nine feet long—almost the length of a car.

The aforementioned facts are true for all of us, and yet these real facts make us the unique individuals that we are. I believe we are created in the image of God, not to be like each other, but to be God-like! It is not our differences from others that make us powerful and therefore Unstoppable. It is the likeness we have with God that has been given to us by God.

You Were Created in the Image of God

The Bible, which is the number-one selling book of all time, tells us in Genesis 1:26–28 (NKJV):

> Then God said, "Let Us make man in Our image, according to Our likeness; and let them have dominion over the fish of the sea and over the birds of the air and over the cattle and over all the earth and over every creeping thing that creeps on the earth." God created man in His own image, in the image of God He created him; male and female He created them. God blessed them, and God said to them, "Be fruitful and multiply, and fill the earth, and subdue it; and have dominion over the fish of the sea and over the birds of the air and over every living thing that moves on the earth."

God created man and woman in His image, gave us dominion over every living thing on earth, and our parents and generation after generation before us have continued the process of making each of us unique. I believe that our individual and collective uniquenesses are designed to serve a purpose, a higher purpose—a God purpose that will benefit humankind.

I want to encourage you to believe that God created you. He didn't just create you—He created you in His own image. How powerful is that? If you will believe this, you will have a chance at reaching your full God-given potential. You will live as one who has a revelation that you have a 1% difference that no one else has.

Allow me to point out a few things about the Genesis of YOU!

- You were created in the "image" of God to image Him in your life.

- You were created in the "likeness" of God to be like Him. To be created in the "likeness" of God means to be supernaturally endowed by God to do what He does.

- The first act of God after He created male and female was He "blessed them." You may not know this, but YOU have been blessed by God. He blessed you before you did anything to be blessed. The purpose of God blessing us is not just so we can be blessed but also so we can be a blessing to others around us.

- God blessed you to be "fruitful." That literally means God blessed you to PROSPER. How does a person become fruitful? She plants seeds. As you Discover, Develop, and Deploy Your 1%, you will have the privilege to sow into other people's lives with the greatness that is in you.

- God blessed you to "multiply." Multiply means to REPRODUCE. You were put on the earth to reproduce God's greatness in you. The more you realize Your 1% and what it is that you uniquely bring to the world as you develop yourself, you will add great value everywhere you go. Guess what happens when you add more value? You become more valuable! Guess what happens when you become more valuable? You are rewarded for the value that you bring.

- God blessed you to "fill the earth." That means to replenish. The way I describe replenish is to become an Energy Producer! In life, you will either be a giver or a taker, a problem or a problem solver, a negative or positive person. The bottom line is you will either be an Energy Producer or an Energy Demander. God blessed you to Produce whatever is needed based on the need and the 1% you have to meet the need.

- God blessed you to "subdue the earth." This means to bring it under subjection through discipline. That happens by you bringing yourself under the discipline and training of God so you can have authority with your 1% to subdue the earth. You have to learn to follow so you can lead, because if you think you are too big to follow, you are too small to lead. If you can't subdue yourself, you will not have much success in subduing anything.

- God blessed you to "have dominion." Dominion means to RULE! God wants you to be a ruler of the earth, operating on the earth like He does in heaven.

Your 1% was given to you by God so you could do what He does—Prosper, Reproduce, become an Energy Producer on the earth, and have the Self-Discipline so you can Rule and Reign the earth!

You Are Unique

My precious wife, Sheila, has a twin sister. They look alike, sound alike, and have many of the same mannerisms. As much as they are alike naturally and at the cellular level, they are independently unique. The identical twin phenomenon happens when a single fertilized egg splits in two after conception. Because the two individuals form from a single zygote, their DNA is indistinguishable and yet . . . they have different, distinctive, and unique fingerprints. How can two people be so alike yet be so uniquely different? It's the 1% Factor!

We are just beginning to learn about all the ways in which we are unique. The entire process associated with genetic mapping and replication is incredibly complex yet extremely precise. You are not only unique in your physical being but also that you were born into the world when and where you were born.

The Shapers of Life

Nobody but you has been born in exactly the same location at exactly the same second, and nobody but you will die in exactly the same place at the same moment. Nobody but you will live in exactly the same life span that you will live, or walk out the steps that you will walk during your lifetime.

Throughout your life, you will walk where no other person has ever walked—precisely. You will encounter a sequence of people and objects that no other person will encounter in the exact sequence and time frame. You will eat different foods and drink different kinds and quantities of liquids, as a composite, than any other person, not only in quantity and quality but also in sequence and location of consumption.

Everything about your life span and your life's journey is one of a kind.

Life first shapes us, but as we develop our 1%
we become empowered to shape life.

Environment

Your environment shapes you. Yet another interesting aspect of genetics research is a fairly recent finding that you and I and every other person are in some type of gene pool. Some of us have highly varied gene pools, which allows for greater diversity in our 1% individuality. These variations impact such things as our skin color and tone as well as the health of the individualized functioning of our brains and bodies.

Heritability

The degree to which an organism's genes contribute to a complex trait is called heritability. This measurement is relative, no pun intended. The more stable the environment, the higher the percentage degree of heritability in any one gene pool. For example, access to good nutrition in a country or region produces a consistently higher percentage degree of heritability for certain traits, such as height, than the uncertainty of nutrition in another country or area, which has a lower percentage degree of heritability for height and other traits. Your environment impacts the genes that you will pass on to the next generation, at least to some degree.

This means that you have some factors in your life that are related to the uniqueness of your family tree and others related to the specific location in which you were born, grew up, and spent most of your time. As you begin to think about your 1%, remember: Our family of Origin gives us our life lessons by default or by design. Then we spend the rest of our lives either building upon them or trying to overcome them.

I want to encourage you to understand that you didn't have a say about what your parents passed to you genetically. But you do have a say about what you are going to do with your genetics. You cannot control everything that has happened to you or around you, but you can control what happens in you and through your 1%!

A Force of Nature and Nurture

The nature-or-nurture debate has raged for more than a century. Now, the conclusion is increasingly this: both nature (genetically fixed factors) and nurture (variable environmental factors and learned traits) are involved in varying degrees in any one individual. There are many forces that go into shaping who we are and who we can become. Think about gravitational pull. We know that our bodies are mostly water, which means that our physical bodies are subject to gravitational pull from the moment of conception in the watery wombs of our mothers. This gravitational pull is linked to the sun and moon, evidenced so clearly in the ebb and flow of ocean tides. This gravitational pull is generated by every heavenly body given its precise location at the precise moment of your birth and onward.

I'm not talking about astrology here. This is astronomical science. The physiology of your body is determined in part by the gravitational pull of all the stars in the heavens, and all of their unseen planets associated with them, on your body that has a precise amount of fluid and exists in a precise location of the earth in any single moment. Granted, the gravitational pull of a star system hundreds of light-years away is almost infinitesimal, but in today's mind-boggling world of technology, *infinitesimal* may just mean "not measurable yet."

The Incredible YOU!

YOU are the most important shaper of your life. We have many influences that can shape us, but WE must take responsibility for shaping ourselves so we can shape the world we want.

There is a story about a pastor who was preparing for his weekend sermon in his home office. His preteen son kept interrupting him, and the pastor was not making much progress on his message. As his son came into his office one more time looking for something fun to do, the pastor reached into a magazine bin he had next to his desk. He opened one of the magazines and found a picture of a world. He had a thought: he tore the page out of the magazine that had a picture of the world on it and tore it up into pieces like a jigsaw puzzle. He said, "Son, I have a game for you. I am giving you what looks like torn-up pieces of paper, but what they are is pieces to a puzzle. The puzzle is a picture of a world, and I want you to go into the kitchen and put the world together by fitting all the pieces together. When you finish, come and get me and I will give you a quarter!"

The son was very excited to take the challenge and hurriedly gathered the pieces from his father and left the room. The pastor was excited because he knew he would have at least some undisturbed minutes to finish his message.

Within five minutes his son returned with a big smile on his face. He said, "I've solved the puzzle, Dad!" As the father looked at the world perfectly fitted together, he asked the son, "How did you do that so quickly, Son?" The son answered, "Well, Dad, on the other side of the world was a picture of a man. And as I pieced the man together, the world came together!"

Piecing Your 1%

Piecing your 1% together is what this book is all about! My goal is to help you put the pieces of your 1% together to reveal the part of you that nobody in the world has, just like your fingerprint.

Think about it. If nobody in history has ever had your fingerprint and nobody in the future ever will, what is it about you that you bring to the world that nobody else ever has?

Every chapter of this book you hold in your hand is a piece that, when put together to create a whole, will reveal your 1%. In Chapter 4, you will learn about your Think, Be, Do and how your Thinking will determine how you will Be, and that how you will Be will determine what you uniquely Do in and with your life. In Chapter 5, you will learn about your Core Values, those things that matter most to you that shape who you uniquely are. Once you choose and know what you value most, you can begin to live a life that matters most. In Chapter 6, you will learn about the importance of your Leadership and how leading yourself is the most important thing you will ever do.

In Chapter 7, you will learn about your T-N-T. To be Transactional or to be Transformational, that is the question. In Chapter 8, we will explore the power of your Life Sentences. These are the things we say that sentence our lives for better or worse. In Chapter 9, we will reveal strategies for Winning at Life with your 1%. In Chapter 10, we will talk about Blind Spots that keep your 1% from operating at full force.

As the pieces of your 1% begin to come together, you will see not only that YOU ARE AN UNSTOPPABLE FORCE but also that your 1%, Your Divine Fingerprint, is what gives you the power to be an Unstoppable Force! When the pieces of your 1% come together, your world will come together like never before!

The Importance of Your 1%

Why the emphasis on being unique? Why is it so important to know your 1%? There are two main reasons.

First, I want you to realize how incredible you are. You are "fearfully and wonderfully made" by God to be like Him! There has never been a YOU in the world. The world is waiting on your 1% so that with what you bring to the world, the world gets better!

Second, your 1% really is your X Factor for Success! As my mentor Zig Ziglar said, "Man was designed for accomplishment, engineered for success and endowed with seeds of greatness." Nobody else was made just like you because nobody else has exactly your purpose on this earth.

Leaders are change agents
who make any change possible.

You bring to every relationship, every encounter, and every experience a unique perspective and a unique set of abilities. You have been designed, engineered, and endowed by God to bring an expression of God to the world that the world has never seen. In other words, you have been downloaded by God, with something from God to give others that no one else has ever had— evidenced by your fingerprint. Could it be that your fingerprint is on your fingertip because what you leave as an imprint is a piece of God you have been given to touch the world?

My challenge to you is to accept and explore your uniqueness, discover your 1%, and then be intentional about the unique imprint you make on the world around you. By doing this, you can deploy your greatness to others around you and you can live a life of purpose and significance.

This book has the tools you need to Discover, Develop, and Deploy Your 1%. I am excited you have decided to take this journey. The world is going to be a better place because of YOU!

THINK, BE, DO

THINK: Discover

What comes to mind when you think about your 1% Factor? Write down the specifics.

Can you identify several ways in which you know you are unique and different from others?

What influences have shaped your life most up to this point?

BE: Develop

Define the specifics of your uniqueness to your current understanding.

DO: Deploy

Be intentional about leaving your 1% imprint in your extended circle of influence.

4

Your Think, Be, Do

*How you Think, Be, Do in life
will determine what you Have in life.*

At fourteen feet tall, it has been called one of art history's greatest masterpieces of all time. The year was 1501 when the Overseers of the Office of Works of the Duomo, commissioned then-twenty-six-year-old Michelangelo to create a statue of David. He was not the first one to be given the commission. In fact, one hundred years before Michelangelo, the assignment was given to Donatello, who never made any progress, and over the next several decades, two other artists were given the opportunity, but both failed. The massive block of Carrara marble found what seemed to be its final resting place in the yard of the cathedral's workshop. When Michelangelo encountered it, it was covered with dirt and partially overgrown with weeds.

Soon the massive piece of unused, dull marble was cleaned and the work on *David* had finally begun. For two years, Michelangelo hammered and chiseled his Think, Be, Do out of a shapeless piece of stone into the beginnings of a matchless work of art! For two more years, he sanded and polished until the statue was complete.

In 1504, after a four-day procession, the *David* was placed in front of the Palazzo della Signoria, the main government building in Florence, facing Rome, as the symbol of the Florentine Republic in its struggle against tyrants who had or would seek to conquer it. (This would be akin to placing it in front of our Capitol building in Washington, D.C.)

When Michelangelo was asked how he was able to create such a masterpiece, he said he was able to Think *David* and not just imagine a man carved out of a piece of marble, so he removed everything that he did not Think was *David*!

Michelangelo's *David* is not just a profound masterpiece of art but is also a way of Thinking, Being, and Doing, representing an artist, but more profoundly, a republic.

Lessons from Michelangelo

For many years, I have been developing a concept: THINK, BE, DO. Those three words capture the very essence of life's change process. You can choose to implement intentional change through a strategic process versus just letting life happen. Let's look at how Michelangelo may have applied Think, Be, Do without even knowing it.

Think: Vision

For a hundred years, the Overseers of the Office of the Duomo wanted a sculpture of David. Why David? David was the biblical character in the Bible who, in their eyes, best represented the Florentine Republic. One of their primary enemies was Rome. They likened Rome to Goliath, who some scholars say was thirteen feet tall. It is interesting that they wanted a fourteen-foot-tall David! Compared to Rome as Goliath, Florence was David. They had a vision and wanted to find someone who could Think *David* rather than just create a statue of a man out of a massive piece of marble.

When Michelangelo received the commission, he didn't just find the marble in a scrap yard, but he also found it to be hopelessly overgrown by weeds—it was seemingly nothing more than a big rock with dirt all over it. It can be the same in our lives. We have to Think *Vision*. We have to get a picture of the future we want regardless of what is happening in the weeds of life. We have to see beyond the dirt of the circumstances we are in. You may have had family members over the last hundred years who gave up on the Vision/*David* of what could have been. But remember, you have your own Divine Fingerprint! They did not have what YOU have! It all starts with how you Think about YOUR future. It's YOUR Vision! YOU are a masterpiece in the making! Just like *David*, you can break from the marble encasement of your thinking. Like Michelangelo, create a *Vision* of your future over the next two to four years.

What do you see in your future? What kind of job do you want? What kind of marriage do you want? What kind of family life do you envision? Your Vision allows you to see what is possible for yourself.

Be: Mission

What was Michelangelo's Mission? Not to create a masterpiece but to Be who he was! He was young, energetic, a believer. He was confident. He was up for the task, no matter what the task was or how long it took. He was a hard worker, competent, and skilled. He was an artist now assigned the greatest Mission of his life: to Be the Best he could Be! His Mission was secondary to his Vision. He had to Think *Vision of David,* so he could Be Michelangelo the Master!

Your Vision will require you to get a clear picture of what you want in your future, and it will help you Be the person who takes on the Mission to accomplish whatever Vision you have! I want to help you become UNSTOPPABLE! My mission from God is to help you Think, Be, Do life better! Your Mission, if you choose to accept it, is to Be the MASTERPIECE that only YOU can Be.

Mission answers the question: Based on who I am, what am I supposed to do?

To Be Mission means to:

- Be the artist of the Vision you see.

- Decide what it is that you want. Most people get more of what they don't want rather than what they want because they never decide what it is they want.

- Write the Vision and make it plain (Hab. 2:2).

- Take action every day. Our job is to believe. God's job is to do the impossible. But between our belief and God doing the impossible, we must take massive action and do everything we know to do.

Don't quit! Three people quit and gave up their Mission to create a masterpiece called *David* over a period of a hundred years. Michelangelo didn't just take the Mission—he was the Mission in the making! It took a total of four years, every day, hammering and chiseling his way toward Greatness.

Do: Purpose

I love my Webster's 1828 dictionary! Look at the definition Webster gives for *purpose:* "that which a person sets before himself as an object to be reached or accomplished; the end or aim at which the view is directed in any plan, measure or exertion; the purpose always includes the end in view."

I love that definition, and that is exactly what Michelangelo did! He knew what his purpose was, and therefore he knew what was set before him as an objective to be reached. He used his Think to Vision *David* and not just to see a useless piece of stone. He used his Be to carry out the Mission that was before him by Being the Best artist that he could Be and creating a masterpiece called *David*.

Purpose answers the question: Why do I exist, and is what I am doing fulfilling and creating the results for why I am here?

To Do Purpose means to:

- Know why you exist
- Utilize your fingerprint to make a masterpiece
- Exercise your 1% everywhere you go
- Take the first step
- Perform with excellence

THINK + BE + DO = HAVE

As we have seen with Michelangelo, this is a strategic process anyone can use. If you apply it consistently and make it a part of your life's process, it will work and will exceed your expectations. It comes back to choice. Who were Donatello, Agostino di Duccio, and Antonio Rossellino? They were the three men in a hundred-year period before Michelangelo who were commissioned to create *David*! Why did they not succeed? It took one hundred years and three failures for someone to Think, Be, Do on the level that Michelangelo did to achieve masterpiece results!

If you can apply Think, Be, Do to your life, you will be able to produce the Haves that you want. Our Think, Be, Do becomes our modus operandi that produces the results that we want to achieve.

The THINK, BE, DO Model applied to elevating your 1% Factor will provide you a road map to success that produces confidence, personal growth, strength in relationships, and positive financial growth, and I believe it will proactively impact every area of your life.

THINK

Think about the following questions:

Where did you learn to think like you think?

Who taught you to think?

Why do you think in the way in which you think?

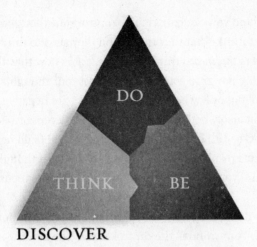

DISCOVER

The goals in Think: Discover are to find out who and what have influenced our thinking and then to understand why we need to elevate our thinking.

A Case for Elevated Thinking

I believe when you elevate your thinking, you elevate your life. How important are our thoughts? When we come into the world as babies, our thoughts are not discovered. In fact, we are able to feel before we are able to think. But at some point in our maturation process, we begin to process words that express thoughts, feelings, and emotions. Acknowledgment of those emotions begins to lead our behaviors and the actions we take. The actions we take form what I call habit forces in our lives, which develop our character. Our character then shapes our destiny.

Control Your Thoughts

You begin to Discover Your 1% when you take ownership of your Thinking. You take ownership of your thinking when you begin to understand you can consciously control your thoughts. Many people just think what they think, and they start to think what they think is *the* way to think, because that is how they think! You have the power to consciously control your thoughts. You can control not only whether your thoughts are negative or positive but also whether or not you want to accept or reject thoughts. One thing is for sure: negative thoughts do not produce positive results! Once you have recognized a thought as negative and you reject it, you empower your 1% to focus on the positive.

Picture it like this: Your thoughts are like a plane approaching an airport. Your mind is the control tower. The landing strip is your heart. As the plane (thought) begins to approach the airport, the pilot radios the control tower (mind) and asks for permission to land. The controller (you) in the control tower (your mind), says, "No!" The plane (thought) is never allowed to land (in your heart). The Bible says in Proverbs 23:7 (NKJV), "As [a man] thinks in his heart, so is he."

Clarify Your Emotions

As you control your thoughts, you clarify your emotions. Dr. Albert Ellis, the "grandfather of cognitive behavioral therapies," and Dr. Aaron Beck, the "father of cognitive behavioral therapy," teach that toxic emotions arise from three negative beliefs:

- *I must do well.*

- *You must treat me well.*

- *The world must be easy.*

We can begin to clarify our emotions when we elevate our thinking:

- From *I must do well* to *I will do my best.*

- From *You must treat me well* to *I will do unto others as I would like them to do unto me.*

- From *The world must be easy* to *I will sow good seed, and I will reap a good harvest.*

Baseline facts:

- Negative emotions evolve out of thoughts of fear.

- Positive emotions evolve out of thoughts of faith.

We elevate our emotions from negative to positive when we elevate our thinking from fear to faith!

Construct Your Words

Words are, of course, the most powerful drug used by mankind.

RUDYARD KIPLING

The fable of the wise servant and the philosopher has an important lesson for us. Xanthus, the philosopher, sent his faithful servant Aesop and told him to bring the best food he could bring for a sumptuous banquet. Aesop went to the market and brought back tongues from all kinds of different animals. He served a full-course dinner. He would serve one tongue with a certain kind of sauce, and then the next course came along, and it was another kind of tongue with a different sauce on it.

Finally, Xanthus was just furious and called Aesop in and said to him, "Servant, I sent you to the market to get the best thing you could find—the best food possible—and you brought us these tongues. Now tell me, what is this madness?"

Aesop, the wise servant, said, "Tongues are the best of all foods. For out of the tongue comes the bond of civilization. Out of the tongue comes the organ of truth and reason. The tongue is the instrument of praise and adoration. What better food could there be than a tongue?"

Xanthus said, "Then tomorrow you go to the marketplace and bring me the worst food you can find."

The next day Aesop served the meal, and he had tongues for every course—served with different sauces, but tongues again.

Xanthus called him aside and said, "I thought I told you to bring the worst food. You've got tongues again. Yesterday it was the best food, and today it is the worst food! Tell me, why are we having tongues as the worst food?"

Aesop the faithful servant said, "Tongues are the instrument of all strife and tension. Tongues! The inventor of lawsuits and slander. Tongues! The organ of error, lies, and all kinds of strife and problems. So I brought you the worst food—that is the tongue."

The best of foods and the worst of foods, this instrument called the tongue.

I believe the tongue is the greatest force in the universe! Our words have the power to elevate our thinking. Your self-talk and the words you speak will determine whether you think negative or positive thoughts and whether you feel bad or feel good. Truly, death and life are in the power of the tongue! How you frame your words will be how you frame your world. Never let anyone's words to you be stronger than the words within you! And let those words that are spoken through you be stronger than the words spoken to you by others.

Think Influencers

Now let's take a look at our Think: Discover process, at who and what has influenced our thinking. Your 1% is shaped by many things, but none is more important than what YOU think! And that is why it is important that you begin choosing your thoughts like never before. I want to encourage you to never give anyone power over your own ability to think. Of course, there are people who can help you elevate your thinking, so with their help, you can elevate your life.

Family of Origin

Our first exposure to thinking was through our FAMILY OF ORIGIN. The vast majority of us think, to a great degree, the way our parents, grandparents, and other influential adults in our childhood taught us to think by their attitudes, actions, words, behavior, and most significantly, overall life example. Our schoolteachers, aunts, uncles, pastors, and even our Sunday school teachers influenced us at an early age. The places we lived, the political environment, and memorable experiences we had growing up also influenced the way we think. These and other influences molded our thought process as we grew and matured. As adults, we carry these mind-sets with us into our new relationships, atmospheres, opportunities, and responsibilities, consciously and unconsciously.

I encounter very few people who think about HOW they think. They simply take for granted the fact that they do think, are thinking, will continue to think, and that to a degree, their thinking is "just fine."

The true foundation of achieving optimal success through elevating your 1% is intentionally making a choice to change the way you think. Everyone can benefit by changing their thought processes. Until you think at an elevated level about the various aspects of your life, your job, your relationships, and your purpose, you cannot experience the success you are destined to HAVE by *being* and *doing* life at an elevated level.

Elevated Thinking is a constant choice that must be implemented to move beyond THINK to the realization of BE. It is a lifelong journey, not a final destination. Elevated Thinking is a new, challenging way of life that will serve you throughout your life as you choose to implement it daily on your journey.

The great news is, you can elevate your thinking in whatever area of life you choose!

Past Experiences

Past experiences also influence our thought processes. These are defining moments we have chosen to allow in by building boundaries in our lives. Most of us have had good, bad, pleasant, unpleasant, winning, and losing experiences. These experiences are reflected in our current decision-making processes and mind-sets.

When you had an experience, you logged it in your memory as good or bad, pleasant or unpleasant, fun or boring, winning or losing, and so on. Without you even realizing it, that particular experience became a defining moment! Mentally, you used that experience to restrict you by establishing unseen boundaries. Some experiences are associated with pain and agony while others are associated with joy and exhilaration. Have you ever stopped to think that some of your experiences may be incorrectly categorized?

Remember, the greatest power you will ever have is the power of choice. Choose to take even the slightest moment and turn it into momentum to create your miracle!

The accuracy of a memory is very important. The evaluation of the past experience is just as important. Why? Because the way in which you remember your past determines to an extent the choices and decisions you will make, consciously or unconsciously, about your future.

Just because you have gone through a plethora of life experiences does not qualify you to be truly experienced. You become experienced when you have grown and learned from your experiences.

Past experiences can be a real stumbling block for people. People use negative experiences as constant reminders for why they can't achieve, why they can't accomplish, why they can't ever overcome, and why they are unworthy to be successful at the level representing their true ability. You can start today to elevate your thinking by taking your worst moments and making them work for your good. This is how you create unstoppable momentum and make any moment a miracle moment. Remember, as we discussed in Chapter 1, a miracle moment is when we make the choice to define the moment rather than letting the moment define us.

Alignments

Another influence affecting your thought process is your relationships. We take on the ideas, attitudes, and perceptions of those around us. To an extent, we take on the thinking of others because we share experiences with others. The choice of those experiences—from retreats and vacation destinations to books we read, music we listen to, churches we attend, and movies we see—is coupled with an evaluation of experiences that very often includes the comments and insights gained from friends, mentors, and family members.

Relationships are important. Having the right relationships is most important. I call this alignment. The most important aspect in life is WHO you are in alignment with because this is the determining factor of all success. No one succeeds alone. We need other people, and other people need us. God intended it to be that way.

If you have been struggling in finding success or you want to be more successful, look first at who you are aligned with. Who are you in relationship with at the job? What is the basis for your friendships, and how influential are they in your life? Who do you listen to? To whom do you turn for information? You see, the people you choose to align your life with reveal how you think.

As alignment is the foundation for success, who you are in alignment with can be the difference between success and failure. Jim Collins, an author of the book *Good to Great*, says that who is on the bus is more important than where the bus is going.

The takeaway here is it is more important to have the right people in your life than to be surrounded by just any people. If you have the right people in your life, you will ultimately achieve more success because you will develop your 1%. You become, in part, a product of who you go through life with!

Who are the right people to align your life with? People who:

- Love and accept you

- Believe you

- Motivate you

- Challenge you

- Have your best interest in mind

- Still believe in the best in you when your worst has been displayed

Who are the wrong people to align your life with? People who:

- Don't love you

- Tolerate you and do not celebrate you

- Don't value the things that matter most to you

- Dishonor you or those you care about

- Are negative

- Discourage you

The case for alignment is found throughout the Bible:

> Bad company corrupts good morals. (1 Cor. 15:33)

> If any two of you shall agree on earth concerning anything that they ask, it will be done for them by My Father in heaven. (Matt. 18:19)

> Do not be unequally yoked. (2 Cor. 6:14–18)

> Behold how good and pleasant it is for brethren to dwell together in unity . . . for there the Lord commands a blessing . . . life evermore. (Ps. 133:1–3)

Alignment in an elevated thinking process includes choosing your family. Though it may be true that we can't pick our parents, we can choose our family. I call this Family of Choice. I believe it is the strongest form of relationship. If you are married, your spouse is an example of Family of Choice.

None of us had a choice as to who our parents were or who our brothers or sisters would be. We didn't decide who our grandparents were going to be, or our aunts or uncles. We all have a family of origin.

For some, the Family of Origin is or was a positive, loving, life-giving, encouraging, healthy, happy, and well-rounded functional experience. For others, the opposite is true. It is, or was, negative, discouraging, unhealthy, perhaps shattering, abuse laden, or some type of addictive environment. Family of Origin for them was a very dysfunctional experience.

The revelation of Alignment is that regardless of the functional or dysfunctional family of origin experience, you can CHOOSE who you want to align your life with! You can CHOOSE a Family of Choice!

I am not saying to not associate with your family and your relatives. I encourage you to become an influential leader in your family of origin as you grow in recognition of your 1%. However, I am pointing out that with an elevated way of thinking about yourself, you can choose a new family that provides the encouragements, disciplines, positive instruction, and loving relationships you need to succeed in your next level.

Elevate Life Church in Frisco, Texas, is known for its leadership culture. Leadership, core values, encouragement, positive reinforcement, servant leadership, self-leadership, and family are core aspects of its culture. Aligning with the culture of a place like Elevate Life Church would be aligning with a Family of Choice—choosing to accept the people and the culture because they are elevating your thought processes and encouraging growth of your 1%.

Alignment with mentors, coaches, instructors, challenging relationships, and loving relationships are important to your growth and success. I have mentors and coaches who speak into my life daily. Most of these are what I call mentors from a distance. I read books. I have a learning agenda. I want to know what I know, and I want to know what I don't know. I don't want to go through life unaware of my shortcomings. I work on myself daily. I seek out mentors, and I seek out mentors from a distance to help me learn, grow, change, and elevate my thinking. I encourage you to do the same.

Who you align your life with will determine
your next level up—or down.

You can choose whoever you want to be your mentor. You can learn from anyone, and they can help you Discover different and exciting aspects of your 1%—the greatness you have. Being unique means you have greatness. Most people assume that *great* means "to be famous or powerful." I love Webster's simplest definition for *Great*: "beyond normal." The GREAT life is a life in motion toward the goal of excellence.

Lots of people I meet want to believe they can be great, and they can. YOU CAN! Some hope to become great someday. But being great isn't about being famous or powerful. Being great and having greatness is to understand who you are, to be confident and not arrogant, to strive for excellence instead of perfection, and to live a life on purpose that matters most. More simply stated, that's living your 1%!

BE

What happened yesterday, last week, last month, last year is over. You can't rewrite history. But you can learn from yesterday and live today with excellence to write and create a better future. It starts with the way you THINK and transitions into how you want to BE.

Who do you want to BE? What does that look like to you? Where will it take you? How will you accomplish it? Why?

The answers to these questions and more are found in the BE process of the THINK, BE, DO Model. As you are further into your journey of THINK: DISCOVER, you can begin to DEVELOP the BE of your 1%.

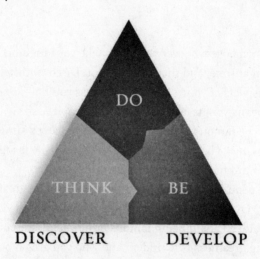

Things to BE Developed

In the development of your 1%, there are certain qualities I believe are important to DO and HAVE a purpose-filled life. It is not to say you don't exhibit or integrate these qualities in your life today. But as you Discover more about your 1%, and endeavor to Develop specifics of BEing your 1%, these traits and qualities will be elevated in your life.

Character

Character is one of the attributes or features that make up and distinguish an individual. In developing your uniqueness and elevating your 1%, your character will mature into an ethical and moral person of excellence. I have found being a person of high character is best achieved by being the best me all the time. I am not proposing that I am perfect. I am not challenging you to be perfect. I am simply stating that anything I decide is worth doing is best accomplished by being the best I can be. So whatever I do, I simply bring my best with me and always do the best I can do in the things I choose to do.

Consistency

Consistency is a result of developing character. In being the best me, I choose to be consistent. I choose to be faithful to the people, the organizations, and the purposes I have chosen to be part of my life. I choose to be the best me in all things I choose to do, thus being consistent and faithful in my thoughts, words, actions, and deeds. Developing consistency also means I am developing coherence, harmony, reliability, persistence, and steady continuity. I endeavor to be found faithful.

Character is judged by reliability and consistency of thought and action. If I am to have strong character, I will be persistent in being the best me, I will be reliable and have steady continuity in thoughts, words, actions, and deeds. I can't be one way part of the time and another way at other times. I choose to be consistent and persist through my challenges to become the best me in all I choose to be part of, wherever I am, and regardless of who's watching.

Trust

Trust can happen only as a result of consistency, faithfulness, and good character and is another quality trait that must BE DEVELOPED to the fullest extent possible. *Trust* by definition is "assured reliance on the character, ability, strength, or truth of someone"—"one in which confidence is placed." Depend. Hope. Believe.

I found the best starting point to developing trust was to trust myself to be the best me. Until I can trust myself, have confidence in myself, believe in myself, and depend on myself, I cannot produce trust for others, nor can I depend on others to trust me, or me them.

Intimacy

Intimacy is developed with others by opening your heart and life with an INTO—ME—SEE attitude. Often misunderstood, Intimacy can also be called authenticity. People who struggle with intimacy often have a hard time being real, being authentic. It is so easy for all of us to wear masks, to hold back positive emotion, because we may be misunderstood. Intimacy or authenticity issues could be a result of fear of failure or fear of acceptance. What's holding you back from being authentic?

Choose to talk about things that need to be dealt with so you develop intimacy in your life by dealing with the pains that limit you. I want to challenge you to GO THERE! *Go where?* you might ask. Open up your heart even if you've been hurt. Open your mind even at the risk of being misunderstood. Be an open book with your life even though you may have some dark chapters. Allow people to know the real you so they will benefit from your greatness and you can benefit from their greatness.

Respect

Respect is a gift we give to others when we choose to trust ourselves to do so. Most people say respect is earned rather than given, but that is because they don't trust themselves and they have intimacy issues. Respect is not about trusting others but is instead about trusting ourselves and our own abilities to be intimate—authentic with our own character. When you trust yourself, you can give the gift of respect.

I want to challenge you to develop a trust and intimacy in yourself based on a trust in and intimacy with God that makes trusting others and being authentic with others easy. I want to challenge you to be the kind of person who respects people, not just because you judge them as good people or you force them to earn your respect. This is a mistake many people make. They give respect out of their own judgment, which could be right or wrong, rather than giving respect out of a heart that is motivated by trusting God, being intimate with God, and then trusting in themselves.

Honor

Respect and Honor go hand in hand. Most people judge behavior not as right or wrong alone but in comparison to their own behavior. Whatever you don't honor, you may dismiss and therefore cannot benefit from. This is what makes honor so important. Even though you may not agree with something, you can still honor it. Develop honor.

Love

Love is only possible when Intimacy and Respect have been developed. Respect is the breeding ground for Love, but to develop Love, you have to be capable of intimacy. Without the capability to be intimate or authentic with God first, yourself second, and then others, you are incapable of respecting and loving yourself, so Loving others only occurs at a surface level.

To develop Love, I want to encourage you to become a Great Lover! Great Lovers don't love people the way they love them back. Great Lovers love people the way they need to be loved. One of the greatest human needs every person has is to be loved. If you will choose to love people the way they need you to love them, you will develop your own ability to love and you will develop a capacity to be greatly loved by others.

Relationship

There are no great relationships without love. Great relationships don't just happen. Great relationships have to be valued, fought for. They happen in what I call a No-Offense Zone. You cannot be a person who is easily offended and ever have great relationships. That's why the Bible says love will cover a multitude of sins.

In Proverbs 10:12 (NKJV), "Hatred stirs up strife, But love covers all sins." And again in 1 Peter 4:8, "And above all things have fervent love for one another, for 'love will cover a multitude of sins.'" This is one of my favorite scriptures.

In Psalms 119:165 (NKJV), the Bible tells us, "Great peace have those who love Your law, And nothing causes them to stumble." Most relationships dismantle as a result of strife, offense, or hurt that lead to unforgiveness and brokenness.

I want to challenge you to develop great relationships by Discovering, Developing, and Deploying your 1% Factor. What that means is, by you identifying your unique 1% and bringing it to other people, you will have great relationships.

People who decide to be 1%ers choose to develop themselves and become the kind of person that they would want to have a relationship with. I want to be the kind of person I would want to have a relationship with, so I will develop my 1% Factor to be the kind of person others will want to be in a great relationship with.

If you want to have Great Relationships, you have to become great at two things: you have to be a great forgiver and a great apologizer.

Quality-Filled Life

A quality-filled life is possible because Great Relationships are developed and maintained. The way to have a quality-filled life is to:

- Be a person of Character

- Be a faithful and consistent person

- Be an authentic person who develops intimacy

- Be a person who gives the gift of respect

- Be a Great Lover

- Be the kind of person you would want to have a relationship with so you develop Great Relationships

Be a 1%er. Be someone who develops your 1% Factor, and you will be a 1%er. That is what makes a quality-filled life possible.

Pattern for a Quality-Filled Life

Faithfulness is the breeding ground for Trust.

Trust is the breeding ground for Intimacy.

Intimacy is the breeding ground for Respect.

Respect is the breeding ground for Love.

Love is the breeding ground for Relationships.

Relationships are the breeding ground for a Quality-Filled Life.

Developing your 1% takes time, energy, and consistency. As I have said, this is a process, a journey, that will lead to a destination. There is an inertia to the old normal-thinking operational mode in your life. This can be overcome by renewing your mind, building alignments, being consistent, and choosing to elevate your thinking about "being the best me." Your old way of thinking, which led to your old way of doing, will now become a new process in your life, which leads to a different way of being.

On the other hand, there is the potential for frustration when you're trying to embrace a new process, feeling like you fall short, and the desire to give up and do it the old way shows up with a vengeance. This too can be overcome by renewing your mind daily, choosing to "be the best me" consistently. If you make a mistake or fall short, dust yourself off and start anew.

We all make mistakes. The challenge is to be the best consistently. When a mistake occurs or poor judgment is displayed, apologize, commit to do better next time, and start over. Don't cover up the mistake. Recognize it, apologize, and move forward with excellence, learning from the mistake to minimize future occurrences.

Let's assume for now that you are my personal or corporate client. I provided you the foundational information on THINK: DISCOVER. You have completed your initial discovery process, and you are working through your BE: DEVELOP process. You're now ready to move to the DO: DEPLOY process.

DO

Today many people I encounter are more concerned about their list of things to do than they are about developing character or refining their thought processes. We are a doing culture. The truth is, what you do will flow from your thoughts and character whether you are intentional about the process or not. My challenge to you is NOT just doing but to do as an outgrowth of intentional pursuit of your 1%.

DO: DEPLOY is a result of having elevated thinking in your discovery process and in developing your elevated BE. As you THINK and BE, you can DO your greatness, bringing forward your uniqueness to the world around you.

Deployment is NOT just about doing. It's about doing with excellence. Think of deploying with excellence in the following ways:

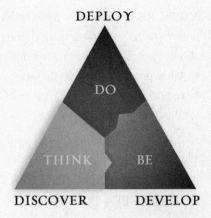

- Deploy Your Values. The more clearly defined your values are, the stronger their influence. The stronger your values, the greater your internal motivation toward aligning your behavior with your ideals. Remember, your values attract what is valuable to you!

- Deploy Your Vision. Your vision is what generates PASSION in you. Show the world the masterpiece that you see and help them to sculpt their own *David*!

- Deploy Your Potential. You may think you are maxing out your potential, but the world can benefit so much more from your 1%! Reaching your full God-given potential is your highest calling.

- Deploy Your Alignments. Alignment before Assignment. Who are you aligned with? Serve the specific family members, friends, customers, and coworkers God has put in your life. It is your ROLE to serve them with consistency and excellence.

- Deploy Your Gifts. Know what you know, and know what you don't know. Establish your learning agenda to grow your knowledge. Find ways to give your knowledge to others. Know what you are good at—and do that. Initiate your own growth. Initiate new ways to serve. Invest in YOU so you can make a deposit in others.

Your 1% Factor that elevates your life to the lofty realm of GREATNESS is reflected in this equation:

THINK + BE + DO = HAVE

One last thought about Michelangelo. His Think, Be, Do caused him to Have a masterpiece called *David*! But not only that, in 1508, at age thirty-three, he was also commissioned by Pope Julius II to paint the ceiling of the Sistine Chapel. He agreed to do it if he could, in his words, "do as he liked." Because of his knowledge of scripture, he was given total freedom, and four years later in 1512, he had completed 343 figures painted on the ceiling.

Pope John Paul II said of it:

> It seems that Michelangelo, in his own way, allowed himself to be guided by the evocative words of the Book of Genesis which, as regards the creation of the human being, male and female, reveals: 'The man and his wife were both naked, yet they felt no shame.' The Sistine Chapel is precisely—if one may say so—the sanctuary of the theology of the human body. In witnessing to the beauty of man created by God as male and female, it also expresses in a certain way, the hope of a world transfigured, the world inaugurated by the Risen Christ.

THINK, BE, DO

THINK: Discover

How did the story about Michelangelo inspire you?

What did you Discover about the Think Influencers?

Make a list of your alignments. Identify three people who should be on your list.

What three things do you need to do to elevate your thinking?

BE: Develop

Implement the Success Triad in your Thinking Process.

Of the Things to Be Developed, what one do you need to work on the most?

Memorize the Pattern for a Quality-Filled Life and seek to follow it.

DO: Deploy

Begin to deploy one identified value to your immediate sphere of influence.

What good can you identify that you Have when applying the Think, Be, Do strategic process?

5

Your Core Values

*When you find out what matters most, you
can begin to live a life that most matters.*

When I was fifteen, we moved to New Orleans, Louisiana, and
unbeknownst to me, the public schools in New Orleans were
all-boy or all-girl schools.

The year was 1975. To find myself in an all-boys school was a
nightmare. No girls—no way! I came home the first day and
asked my parents, "Do you know there are no girls in this
school?" I couldn't believe it! The good news is, I didn't have to
stay there long. We moved thirty miles east of New Orleans to a
town called Slidell. I remember one night after we had moved
there, I was watching *The Tonight Show* when Johnny Carson
said, "Slidell, Louisiana . . . the fastest-growing city in America."
I did not know that. And now, I lived there.

The first day of school, I noticed very quickly that Slidell was a
NORMAL school with both boys and girls attending. I felt alive
again! The basketball coach approached me and asked me if I
played basketball. I told him I did. I was 6'3" and weighed about
175. I have often joked that I was so skinny that when I stuck my

tongue out, I looked like a zipper! I was surprised when the coach invited me to sit on the bench with the team that night. He wanted me to get a firsthand view of the Slidell Tigers' cross-town rival, the Salmen Spartans. I was excited to be on the bench to watch the game and was already envisioning myself on the court when it happened . . .

What caught my eye was not the game between rivals, but a cheerleader on the other side of the court! I turned to the guy next to me on the bench and asked, "Who is that?" He quickly said, "That's Sharla. . . . She has a boyfriend, but there is one on the other end of the floor that looks just like her. Her name is Sheila." I couldn't believe it! There were two of them! Identical twins! I decided at that moment, "One might be taken, but the other one is mine."

After the game that night, everyone went to the local hangout, McDonald's. When I arrived, the girl I had seen was already seated with her cheerleader friends.

I immediately walked up to the table and introduced myself. It was as if her friends knew I wanted to get to know her because immediately they began to giggle and got up and left the table. I asked her if I could sit down. She said YES! I then asked her if she would like a Dr. Pepper. She said—yes! After a few minutes passed, she asked, "Why did you ask me if I wanted a Dr. Pepper?" I said, "Because I am from Dallas, and all girls in Dallas like Dr. Pepper!" I found out later that she had always hated Dr. Pepper.

As we began to talk, I asked her if she had some school yearbooks. She said she did. At that point, I invited myself over to her house to see them. She accepted my invitation, and we went to her house.

We had been there for about thirty minutes talking and looking at yearbooks when I said to her, "I really don't care about yearbooks. I just wanted to get to know you!" She said, "Okay, I'm good with that!" I then said, "I want to start by saying, I am a born-again, spirit-filled Christian." She looked at me like she had just seen a ghost and walked out of the room. At fifteen, I had decided what mattered most to me. It was my relationship with God. I had decided because God mattered most to me, I would only date girls who had that same Core Value—even though I did not know to call what mattered most to me a Core Value yet. So, when she left the room, I thought I had freaked her out or she just wasn't interested, and I prepared to leave. As I was about to leave, she and her mother came walking back into the room, and her mother said, "So, you are a born-again, spirit-filled Christian?"

I stuck out my chest that I didn't have and said, "Yes, I am!" She said, "That's wonderful! We have been praying and believing for our daughter to have Christian friends." I cannot even begin to tell you what I felt in that moment! I wanted to say, "I am the answer to your prayers!" I was laughing and shouting on the inside, and on the outside trying to keep my composure. What I really knew was that she was an answer to my prayers. What I knew but did not understand fully yet was that when you know what matters most to you, you attract what is most important to you. Because you know what matters most to you, you begin to make decisions and spend time with people who align with what you value. This was the beginning of my Core Values–based journey that would set a course for my Core Values–based life.

Relationship Is Most Important

One month later, on January 20, 1976, I asked Sheila Wood to go steady with me and be my girlfriend. She was about to answer yes when I said, "Don't answer yet. I've got something I want to show you." I then took out a piece of paper and drew a triangle. I said, "I have this philosophy about how relationships work, and I would like to see what you think about it." On the left-hand side of the triangle, I wrote her name. On the right-hand side of the triangle, I wrote my name. At the top of the triangle, I wrote *God*.

She took a look at my triangle, and I could tell she was both surprised and intrigued. She responded, "Okay."

I said, "This is how I believe our relationship will work best as long as we both choose to be in relationship with each other. If you will be your best for God"—I drew an arrow from her name pointing up to God's name—"and I will be my best for God"—I drew an arrow up from my name to God's name—"we will meet at the top." I explained, "It's not so much about you and me as it is about US and Him! I believe great relationships are built by individuals who put God first." It was at this point that I drew another arrow between our names. I said again, "If we are both our best for God, we will be our best for each other. Our common denominator is that both of us want what God wants for us." I said, "Is that something you agree with?"

With a smile on her face, she said, "Yes!"

Then I said, "There's something else that is important to me—let's always communicate."

She said, "I like to talk."

I said, "I don't just mean talk. Let's make a commitment never to leave each other angry or to stay upset with each other. Let's do our best to talk things out before we leave each other and go our separate ways for the day."

She said, "Okay, I will try to do that."

I explained Ephesians 4:26–27 (NKJV) that says, " 'Be angry, and do not sin': do not let the sun go down on your wrath, nor give place to the devil." I told her, "If we will attempt to Do relationship this way, we will be healthy and the relationship will be the best it can be in our marriage." She said, "I like that and want that as well."

On January 20, 1976, Sheila Wood became my girlfriend. I told her then that I would remember that day and honor her on that day every month for the rest of our lives. From that day forward, we have celebrated our anniversary on the twentieth of every month. As I write this, today is November 20, 2012. We have had 442 anniversary celebrations! I brought my 1% to our relationship before I knew there was a 1%, because I knew what mattered most and have been privileged to live a life that most matters!

I want to emphasize again that I did not know to call what matters most Core Values, but that is what I was focusing on. By emphasizing our individual relationship with God first and then our relationship together second, I was establishing Relationship as my number-one Core Value. By saying, "Let's be our best for God," I was establishing Excellence as a Core Value for our relationship. By saying, "Let's always communicate," I was establishing Communication as a Core Value. By saying, "Let's do our best to talk things out before we leave each other and go our separate ways for the day," I was establishing Conflict Resolution as a Core Value. By choosing to celebrate Sheila on the twentieth of every month, I was establishing Honor as a Core Value in our relationship.

Values Set the Course of Life

I was honored to date Sheila all through high school. What great memories we have of school dances, football games, friends, parties, and the most fun dates you could ever imagine in my 1969 Mustang with a 351 Cleveland engine! She was a cheer-leader, and I was a basketball player, and if I were writing a movie script for how I wanted a relationship to be, it couldn't have been any better. Core Values—I believe in them!

One quick dating story . . .

On our first date, I drove to Sheila's house to pick her up. She looked incredible and, with her bubbly personality, bounced out to my car. As we were walking out, I opened the passenger-side door for her. I then walked around the car and got in on the driver's side. I started the car, reached for her hand, and said, "Let's pray." I prayed a brief prayer over her that went something like this: "God, I thank You for the opportunity to be with such an awesome girl. We just dedicate this night to You. Help us to have a great time. Thank You, God! Amen!" She said, "Amen!" I didn't let go of her hand. I shifted into gear holding her hand. It was AWESOME!

We graduated from high school together and decided to go to Evangel University, where I had a basketball scholarship. For the next four years, we spent most of our free time together. I played basketball, and she was a cheerleader! During our sophomore year, Sheila thought it might be a good idea to date others, and I encouraged her to! I went to my best friend at the time and told him if I wasn't going to date her, then I wanted him to date her, because I wanted the absolute best for her. He asked her out that day!

Long story short, we got back together after a very short period because she decided that along with wanting me, she wanted what I wanted in life. We valued the same things. That was the glue then, and it is the Super Glue now!

We were married in 1982 and have since raised three beautiful, talented, Core Values–based children, and we are now privileged to work together as a family. Core Values set the course for your life in your family and in any business you are ever involved in.

What Are Core Values?

Core Values are the What Matters Most that we live by. They influence EVERYTHING, including:

- The decisions we make

- Our responses to people and situations

- Our commitments to organizational and personal goals

And they:

- Provide direction for our daily behavior

- Are the foundation that will ultimately determine our success

Challenge yourself. Consider your answers to these questions:

- Why is it important to me to live a core values–based life?

- Why is it important to know what I value?

- What do core values do for me?

- What are my top three core values?

I believe there is nothing more important that you can do right now than make the decision to live a Core Values–based life. Why? Because your Core Values—What Matters Most to you—are the most critical piece of your 1% Factor.

There are many things that have influenced who you are right now. Your family of origin, other people's opinions, ideologies and ideas, your defining moments, and your past experiences shape the values that you establish, consciously or unconsciously. It is important to recognize that once you identify what your Core Values are, you have the power to begin to build the kind of life that Matters Most to YOU!

Your core values influence every aspect of your life, affect your sphere of influence, and determine how you handle life's challenges. When you know what you value, you can begin to align everything with those values. What you believe is based on what you value. Who you Do life with is based on what you value. How you make money and what you Do with your money is based on your Core Values.

What Do Core Values Do in Your Life?

Core Values are like the navigational compass on a ship, a GPS on your car, the computer guidance system on an airplane— they are your internal guidance system. Programmed properly, your core values will guide you to success and keep you on purpose. Your Core Values are a part of your unique finger-print, and they empower you to leave your unique imprint everywhere you go and with everyone you meet. They are the foundation of your 1% and the guideposts of your personal GREATNESS!

What's So Important About What's Most Important?

- Core values determine your character.

Someone has said, "Character is who you are when nobody's looking." I believe your character is the real you. The real you is based on what is REALLY important to you. It is the unseen part of you that is eventually revealed in your daily actions.

To do this to the right person, to the right extent, at the right time, with the right motive and in the right way, that is not for everyone, nor is it easy; wherefore goodness is both rare and laudable and noble.

ARISTOTLE

- Core values shape your culture.

Each family, church, or organization has a unique culture. A culture is a created atmosphere (felt presence) shaped by values, attitudes, beliefs, and behaviors. Every culture is established by default or by design.

The same is true for individuals. Your core values shape your personal culture and generate specific outcomes. You CAN change your current position. You CAN become more confident of future outcomes. Your objectives are what drive your outcomes. Objectives that matter are built on a foundation of What Matters Most! My objective at fifteen was to have a relationship with a girl based on what mattered most to me. The outcome I was looking for was a great God-first relationship.

As you begin discovering your core values and develop the objectives based on those values, you will begin to operate in your 1% and achieve the outcomes you desire.

- Core values bring clarity and focus.

They express who you are, what you are about, the way you do things, and what you stand for. The better you understand your 1%, the better you can develop and deploy your greatness as defined by your values.

- Core values communicate what is important.

Communication is a window by which others come to understand our values, as expressed by our words, through our actions, in our body language, and by what we support with our resources including our time and money. Our values are also expressed by how we show up to serve beyond our pay grade.

- Core values influence our behavior.

We cannot behave differently than what we truly believe matters most. Our behavior will reflect what we value. Behave proactively not reactively. Lead from your core. Behave as if what is most important to you . . . is most important.

- Core values are determining factors in life.

When you build a house, you do not stop at the foundation. However, the foundation is the most important part and determines the stability of the house. There is a story in the Bible about two men who each built a house. One house was built on the Rock. The storms raged. The winds blew and beat against the house, and it did not fall because it was built on the foundation of Rock. But the other man built his house on a foundation of sand. When the storms raged and the winds blew, the fall of that man's house was great. It fell because it was built upon a foundation of sand. The builder failed. Your Core Values are the foundation for the kind of life-house you want to build. They determine not only what is in the house but also who is in the house.

• Core values elevate effective leadership.

The most important person you will ever lead is yourself. That is what makes Core Values so important. You can only lead yourself if you know What Matters Most to you! I am convinced that most problems people have stem from not knowing how to lead themselves. Your Core Values will help you lead yourself to Think in a unique way, Be a certain way, and Do specific things that cause you to Have the life you want.

Getting to the Core of Your 1%

Early in my life, I became aware that I was viewed by others as a leader. From the time I was in elementary school, I was a leader amongst my friends. One of the early distinctive differences was my hunger for God. I loved to sit in the front row of the church. I would go forward at every opportunity to pray at the altar. By the time I was nine, I knew I was called into ministry and that I would spend my life leading others to the "light" of God.

Getting to the Core of my 1% was discovered through my relationship with God. I decided early that God mattered most and that every desire, discipline, and decision began to be shaped by my values. Only YOU can decide what is not just at your Core but what is the basis for what you value most.

Through the years, I have dreamed big dreams. Armed with Core Values, I have grown as a leader, and God has helped me to identify all the tension between where I am and where I want to be, to develop strategies for overcoming any obstacles that would keep me from achieving the results I want. I live with a passionate desire to help others with the achievement of their big dreams. As you will see, it is out of my desire to be Core Values based that my own 1% can be maximized.

I have been privileged for decades to operate out of my 1% to help individuals, groups, and companies to set goals, identify problems, implement problem-solving strategies, and stay motivated until stated goals are met. As a Core Values–based leadership strategist, my heart is set to help people reach their full God-given potential.

Along the way, God has helped me to develop and refine my leadership abilities. I have learned a little patience, and I probably need to learn just a little bit more. If I see a goal, I want to get there TODAY, if not sooner. I have learned to help others through Core Values–based leadership to see the problems that need to be overcome.

Embrace the Tension

John Gardiner said, "Most of us plateau when we lose the tension between where we are and where we ought to be." The problems we have are often related to the plateaus in our lives. Our marriage plateaus. Our job plateaus. Our life plateaus. Once anything plateaus, if I lose the tension between where I am and where I need to be, I go into decline. Core Values remind me of what is most important. They have the power to propel me into a hope-filled future, because they keep me focused on what is most important about the future. I've learned to identify more than one strategy for getting to a goal. But the most important stratagem I have learned is that Core Values make goal achievement possible. Once I know what matters most, I can then set goals to achieve the outcome I want.

Some of what I've learned has come from reading and studying leadership. Some of it has come from trial and error. But my best learning has come from being in the middle of something—a situation or circumstance—and doing what needs to be done, when it needs to be done based on what is most important.

What situation are you in right now that is definitely a problem for you? You may not know everything you need to do, but you can do something! You can decide right now what is most important to you. Don't just get to the core of the problem. Get to the Core of YOURSELF! It's there. You will begin to operate in your 1% by first deciding what is most important and then taking action based on what you define.

---

*Leadership and learning
are indispensable to each other.*

JOHN F. KENNEDY

Your 1% Determines Your Value

Have you identified your foremost God-given gift? Have you recognized the propensity you have for making a difference in this world? Are you embracing that trait and developing it?

Everybody is gifted to a degree with being a leader. A person always has the responsibility to lead himself. A married man or father has a responsibility to lead his family. But not everybody is gifted to be an organizational leader.

That doesn't mean there aren't equally fine gifts and traits at the foundation of a person's character. Some people are gifted with a talent for implementation. They can administer another person's vision with a keen eye for detail and follow-through. Some people are gifted with an ability to motivate or encourage through simple acts of kindness, hospitality, or giving. Some people are gifted with an ability to learn and teach. They are able to take in vast amounts of information and digest them into practical application enhanced with divine wisdom.

Now, to a degree, every person is capable of implementation. It is at the core of personal responsibility. Every person is capable of self-motivation. Every person is capable of learning and applying what is learned. But if one of these traits is the foremost gift you have had from birth, then this is the gift you are to Discover, Develop, and Deploy! This is the trait that is at the foundation of your character.

You cannot BE fully who you were created to be unless, and until, you Discover the traits that have been built into you from your birth, Develop and realign those traits with achieving your purpose, and Deploy your 1%.

You probably would not have concluded that I was born to be a leader if you had heard the nicknames my parents had for me when I was a boy. My father didn't call me Champion, which is what I frequently call my son and have called him from his birth. My dad didn't call me Winner. He called me . . . SQUIRREL.

Now imagine growing up with that affectionate nickname from a dad! He'd say to me, "Hey, Squirrel." I'd say, "Hey, Dad."

One day when I was about eleven years old, I asked him, "Why do you call me Squirrel? I look at squirrels running around the yard and park and . . . well . . . I don't exactly see myself like that. Maybe you can tell me what you see."

He said, "Keith, it's like this. You're on this tree branch . . . and then in a flash, you're on the next tree branch. Whooooosh. I think, *There he goes!* And then you don't stay there long. Whooooosh. There he goes! All we see is your tail."

Actually, I liked that. I embraced the nickname Squirrel from that day forward. I am a person who is constantly in motion, constantly exploring the next good option, constantly willing to adjust and adapt if it means improvement. I move quickly and decisively.

When I was a boy, my father would often take me to school in his squad car. He would drop me off on his way to work. When I rode with him, I'd scoot over in the front seat so that I was practically in his lap. I liked to be as close to him as possible. By the time I was in the seventh grade, I was almost as big as my dad. My mother would tell me we looked a little funny riding down the street with me sitting next to my dad, especially in a police car!

The truth was, I loved my dad, and sitting close was my 1% way of saying I love you. The Lord showed me early in life that my father hadn't received affection from his father. He'd received very few verbal or physical expressions of love from any person during his childhood years. My 1% to my dad was the value I brought to him by loving him in a way he had never been loved.

Too, oftentimes, we don't know what value we bring because we don't know what our values are. When we don't know what our values are, we don't know how VALUABLE we are. So rather than understanding that we have a 1% that no one else has, we feel disappointed, disillusioned, and dissatisfied in what we don't get that we want to get from other people. And yet one of the greatest truths ever written says, "It is more blessed to give than to receive."

My mother called me an octopus. I asked her one day, "Why do you call me an octopus?" She said, "Because you are always touching people. If someone comes up to you, you can't help but put your hand on that person."

Actually, I liked Octopus as a descriptor of my life once my mother explained it the way she did! My ability to be affectionate is a part of my 1%. It is an expressed ability to be intimate. One of my personal Core Values that you will see is Relationship. You don't get to have close relationships if you're not willing to be intimate. Many men, especially, have intimacy issues and don't know it. I speak to hundreds of thousands of men every year on this very subject.

I have decided that the combination of being a squirrel and an octopus makes me a fast-moving hugger—eager to touch the lives of as many people as I can. Since I'm being very vulnerable here, I'll tell you that I'm not adverse to that overall metaphor! I love people, and I love to touch and challenge people in some way—physically, emotionally, mentally, or spiritually. That's just my leadership qualities coming out. That relates to my value that I bring to relationships and the ongoing Discovering, Developing, and Deploying of my 1%!

I don't know the nicknames that may have been given to you, but in some way, they may be indicators of a trait in you that pertains to the personal God-given attributes that are part of your 1% Factor for greatness.

Your personality and persona-distinctive traits are a good starting point for you to develop. They are keys to your success. They are the unique traits that, in combination, create your personal brand and imprint you will make in the world.

Embrace your good qualities! Never back away from the good qualities within you. Embrace them and develop them. Own them. Don't ever be reluctant to display them.

I am not at all ashamed to say that I am a swinging-for-the-fence, on-the-go, eager-to-express-affection-and-encouragement, God-serving and faith-filled LEADER! That's who I am. That's the BE part of my life. That's my character. Each one of us has a decision to make as to what is most important based on our personality, call, preferences, and potential to make a difference in the lives of others.

You don't do anyone a favor by playing small. Be who you are, who you are purposed to be, and bring your 1% Factor. Don't deny or diminish the importance of the way God made you.

Positive change will never happen if negative thinking is tolerated.

Know Your Core Values

A lot is said about values in our world today, but in my experience speaking to groups across this nation for more than twenty-five years, I have concluded that the majority of people who readily say, "I am a person with great values!" cannot tell me what their values are. They know they have them, but they've never listed or defined them.

I want to challenge you to know your values—what matters most to you—and to be able to state them clearly. More than twenty years ago, I developed a list of what I considered to be Things that Matter Most. And from that list, I identified my top ten, five of which I will share with you now.

I have five main personal core values. That is not to say there aren't many other things I value—these are just the top five:

1. I value my relationship with God.

2. I value my relationship with my wife.

3. I value my relationships with my children.

4. I value my health and well-being.

5. I value opportunities to contribute my time, my talent, and my treasure.

These five core values are a template for not only how I expect to live my life as a whole but also how I expect to live each day. They drive my daily agenda, my weekly agenda, and my annual agenda. They determine my schedule and the checks I write out of my checking account. It is one thing to have Core Values; it is another thing to LIVE them. I made a commitment a long time ago that every day:

- I spend time building up my spiritual life. My spiritual life is my life. My relationship with God must permeate every other relationship and every task I undertake. I choose daily to serve God in praise, prayer, reading His word, and listening to Him in quiet contemplation.

- I spend time nurturing and nourishing my relationships with my wife and children. They are the template for how my other relationships work.

- I spend time doing what is healthful. This isn't limited to working out and pursuing the best health I can achieve. It means pursuing wholeness—pursuing healthy habits in every area of my life, including:

  Balance in earning and spending
  Balance in work and recreation

Balance in giving and receiving

Balance in spending time alone and time with others

- I spend time developing and contributing my time and my ideas. I look for ways to serve others and to give to help alleviate urgent needs. I want to be a faithful Christian, a great husband, a great father, a whole person, and a GIVER to my coworkers and others who seek information or inspiration from me—every day, for the rest of my life.

The following is a Values List I want to encourage you to use to help you identify Your Values. You may have others you want to add. My goal here is not for you to value the same things I value but rather to help you Know Your Core Values.

Values List

In the right column, check all values that are important to you. In the left column, prioritize your top ten.

PRIORITIZE	VALUE	CHECK
	Peace of mind	
	Friendships	
	Security	
	Retirement	
	Wealth	
	Knowing important or famous people	
	Good health	
	Being in business for yourself	
	Close relationship with spouse	
	Having no problems to deal with	
	Living to an old age	

PRIORITIZE	VALUE	CHECK
	Close relationships with children	
	Spending time with extended family	
	Personal possessions	
	Meeting the right person	
	Traveling to exciting places	
	Meaningful job or career	
	Sense of accomplishment	
	Fame	
	Respect from others (being thought of as a good person)	
	Power	
	Free time	
	Close relationship with God	
	Happiness	
	Contributing time, knowledge, and money to others	
	Generosity	
	Positive attitude	
	Excellence	

Do you know your personal core values?

Can you list them in order of priority?

Does your life reflect the values you have listed? In the order listed?

I know with certainty that few people have ever fully identified their core values. Everyone has values by default or by design. I believe that only a very small percentage by design know what they value and are living according to their values—their 1%.

Knowing your values, those things that Most Matter to YOU, and living them is choosing to live your 1% to the fullest by bringing Your Value everywhere you go.

THINK, BE, DO

THINK: Discover

What are your Core Values?

Are you living what you say your values are?

BE: Develop

Prioritize your Core Values—number one is strongest and so forth.

How can you strengthen weaker identified values?

DO: Deploy

Implement one of your Core Values into your daily process. Monitor the progress of strengthening your character. Record your progress.

6

Your Leadership

Leadership is one of the most observed and least understood phenomena on earth.

— JAMES MACGREGOR BURNS

I have always been fascinated by the subject of Leadership. By the time I was nine years old, I had answered the call of God. I did not know all of what that meant, but I knew I had an insatiable hunger in my heart to follow and please God. I was compelled by God to lead myself to follow Him. For me personally, this is where my Leadership journey began.

My hunger for Leadership stemmed from a desire to be the best I could be. As a child, I began to see very quickly that everyone around me was not necessarily THINKING, BEING, and DOING life this way. Everyone has an opinion about what Leadership is—how, when, where, and why it should be done!

In this chapter, I want to address my own journey of leadership that has led me to Discover-Develop-Deploy my 1%.

Leadership Is . . .

There are almost as many definitions of leadership as there are
books on leadership. In fact, there are 393 current books that
have *lead* or *leadership* in their title. During the last decade, I
have been privileged to be a part of some of the largest business
seminars in the world. I have shared the platform with former
presidents of the United States including Bill Clinton and
George Bush; world leaders Margaret Thatcher, Mikhail Gorbachev, and Benjamin Netanyahu; Super Bowl–winning coach
Tony Dungy and quarterback Joe Montana; military leaders
Colin Powell and General Tommy Franks; America's Mayor
Rudy Giuliani; and financial gurus Suze Orman and Steve
Forbes. I have interviewed and shared the stage with actors Bill
Cosby, Michael J. Fox, Chuck Norris, Jerry Lewis, and Goldie
Hawn. I have met and learned from the best leaders in their
fields from all walks of life.

. . . Learning from the Greatness of Others
My library is filled with some of the best leadership books ever
written. I have been a student of leadership thinkers and gurus
like Peter F. Drucker, Ken Blanchard, Warren Bennis, Stephen
Covey, Dale Carnegie, James M. Kouzes, Barry Z. Posner, Max De
Pree, John P. Kotter, Thomas J. Peters, Jim Collins, Malcolm
Gladwell, W. Edwards Deming, Marcus Buckingham, Tom Kelley,
Daniel Goleman, Brian Tracy, Og Mandino, Bill George, Marshall
Goldsmith, Denis Waitley, Norman Vincent Peale, Napoleon Hill,
and believe it or not, the list goes on and on! My favorite and most
inspiring are Zig Ziglar, Tony Robbins, and John Maxwell.

The reason I mention authors I have read is because leaders
are readers. When you read someone's book, you are reading

the best of them. Read what they have written. Learn from them. Take action on what you read, and add their greatness to your 1%.

. . . Always a Way of Thinking First, that Determines a Way of Being, that Becomes a Way of Doing

The way you Think about God, yourself, others, and everything will determine your Be, or how you are as a person. How you think about God will determine your whole philosophy of life. If you think God is real, then you are going to believe that you were born for a purpose. If you don't think God is real, your sense of purpose will be shaped by that belief. How you think about yourself will shape your Being as it relates to your self-image and your self-esteem. How you think about others will determine your attitude toward them. Your attitude, which springs from your Being, will affect everyone and everything in your life. Your attitude is the hinge that the door of your destiny swings on. Your attitude is YOU! Who you are (BE) as a person, will manifest in your way of Doing life. Your attitude, your behaviors, and the actions you take all start with Your Thinking.

. . . the Capacity of an Individual to Discover Her Passion, Develop Her Vision, and Deploy Her Greatness that Elevates Her Personally and Creates the Ability to Empower Others to Do the Same

This would be my extended version of my own definition of Leadership. Leadership is . . . a lot of things, but it begins with Passion. Passion can be defined as an extravagant fondness, enthusiasm, or desire for anything. We will discuss it through-out this book. It is related to your natural gifts and talents. The fact is that once you discover your Passion, you can begin to develop your Vision, which is the picture of the future you want. As you lead your Passion and Vision, you will deploy your Greatness, which I call your 1% Factor—Your Unstoppable Force!

. . . Discovering That When You Change What Needs to Change for the Better IN You, You Gain the Power to Change What Is Around You

One of the many things I love about Leadership is the discovery that in leading yourself through change, you gain the confidence to understand that anything around you can get better. Often people want their situation to change without changing themselves. They focus on other people's need to change rather than their own need to change. They expect other people to do what they are not willing to do. Leaders are focused on what needs to change within themselves before they ever hope that others will change. And yet, because leaders Think this way, they can have hope that if they can change, others can too. Leaders Think that, if they change, they will be better able to influence positive change in others.

. . . The Art of Ruling Oneself—Spirit, Soul, and Body

"Whoever has no rule over his own spirit is like a city broken down, without walls," as the Bible says in Proverbs 25:28 (NKJV). Ruling your own spirit is inside-out living. It is a lifetime commitment to leading your mind (Thinking), your attitude (Being), and your body (Doing) every day. It is guarding your heart, governing your mind, and guiding your body to do what you want YOU to do. It is relentless correction and direction of self. It is embracing the belief that there is no direction without correction. Normal thinkers struggle with their direction in life because they don't correct themselves enough. If you will correct yourself when you need correction, you will direct yourself when you need direction. As Pietro Aretino said, "I am, indeed, a king, because I know how to rule myself."

. . . Doing What You Don't Feel Like Doing, When It Needs to Be Done

Leadership and maturity go hand in hand. You know you are maturing when you do what needs to be done, when it needs to be done, how it needs to be done. Leaders don't feel their way into action; they act their way into a feeling. You are leading yourself when you don't feel like doing what you know needs to be done but you do it anyway. I can tell you that I never feel like working out—ever! But I believe God has given me my body to serve Him. I believe my body is the temple of God. I work it out when I say, not when it says. I will not give in to my body's cravings and desires. My feelings are subject to what I think. My body is subject to what I choose to do with it. I don't believe the myth of following your heart. Leaders lead with their values, as we discussed in the previous chapter, and their hearts follow. Our bodies are the same way. We have to lead the feel, not feel the lead.

. . . Doing the Most Important Thing You Can Do Every Day!

Leadership is not only doing the most important thing you will do every day, but it is also doing the hardest thing you will do every day. The most important relationship you can cultivate on earth is the relationship you have with yourself. In fact, Jesus, the greatest leader of all time, said, "Love your neighbor as yourself" in Mark 12:31 (NKJV). You have to lead yourself to love yourself. You love yourself when you take care of yourself.

When my children were growing up, I taught them about spaces. Your room is your space. It is a picture of your world in the future. Believe it or not, how you take care of your space is a reflection of how you feel about yourself. I would tell them, "Love yourself enough to know you deserve excellence and that you know what excellence looks like." When they got cars, it was the same way. I would tell them, "Your space is a reflection of you. Value your space because it is your space. Create the space you want to live in; then everywhere you go, you know that space can change, because you are there!"

Leaders lead themselves to create spaces of success. When you lead yourself, you create a path that becomes a trail for others to follow.

. . . Knowing the Difference Between Normal Thinking and Leadership Thinking

Before it is anything else, leadership is a way of thinking. Often, we see others substitute positioning or posturing for true leadership. For example, people who decide to become parents aren't necessarily thinking about leadership. They are thinking about wanting a baby or having a family. But parenting is leadership for better or worse. In my opinion, there is no greater position of leadership and influence than that of a parent. People who go to college and get degrees in education because they want to be teachers aren't necessarily thinking about leadership. In most cases, they want to simply teach. But being a teacher is so much more than just teaching a subject to a class.

People who are gifted as athletes and excel on the collegiate level by achieving scholarships aren't necessarily thinking about leadership. They just love the game they love. They may even go on to play on a professional level, not because they want to be leaders but because they have the talent and the skill and want to get paid well for what they do. Think about Hollywood and the influence actors and actresses have on politics, culture, and morals in our society. When people decide to be actors, are they thinking about leadership? I don't think so. But are they seen as influencers? Yes!

Leadership vs. Normalship

Let's take a look at the difference between how a leader thinks and how a normal thinker thinks. I want to differentiate between leadership and what I call normalship. I believe you'll agree that there are way too many normal-thinking people in leadership positions today.

Look at the list below and rank yourself by filling in a box to the left of center if you think more leadership or to the right if you think more normalship. This exercise is to help you to see what it is to Think Leadership as opposed to thinking normalship. True effective leadership requires elevated thinking!

My challenge to you is not to think this way because of a position you have or are going to potentially have in the future. But the goal is to show you what a leader thinks like using a side-by-side comparison with a normal thinker. Be honest with yourself, and in the end, see if you think more Leadership or more Normalship. The world—your world—needs you to Think Leadership! The effectiveness of your 1% to influence positive change wherever you go is contingent upon how YOU think.

	LEADERSHIP	VERSUS	NORMALSHIP
1	Live with a transcendent cause	□□□□□□	Live with a what's-in-it-for-me? attitude
2	Embrace resistance	□□□□□□	Resist resistance
3	Refuse to be offended	□□□□□□	Exercise your right to be offended
4	Do not gossip	□□□□□□	Gossip if it's true
5	Believe the best when the worst has been displayed	□□□□□□	Believe the worst especially if the worst has been displayed
6	Desire to be your best	□□□□□□	See no need to change
7	Lead yourself first	□□□□□□	Want others to change first
8	See what is possible	□□□□□□	See things as impossible
9	Act into a feeling	□□□□□□	Feel your way into an action
10	Do whatever it takes	□□□□□□	Do whatever is easiest
11	Do more than you are asked	□□□□□□	Do only what is required
12	Love people the way they need to be loved	□□□□□□	Love others the way you love
13	Give generously (above and beyond)	□□□□□□	Give obligatorily (what you have to)
14	Develop your personal greatness	□□□□□□	Despise the greatness in others
15	Practice like it's game time	□□□□□□	Practice like it's practice
16	Exhibit confidence	□□□□□□	Exhibit insecurity
17	Extend mercy	□□□□□□	Pronounce judgment
18	Seek to understand	□□□□□□	Seek to be understood
19	Overcome	□□□□□□	Overwhelm
20	Display a spirit of excellence	□□□□□□	Display a spirit of perfectionism
21	Pro-activate	□□□□□□	Procrastinate
22	Live Core Values	□□□□□□	Live for others' approval
23	Seek victory in adversity	□□□□□□	Become a victim of adversity
24	Focus on self-improvement	□□□□□□	Focus on self-pity
25	Forgive	□□□□□□	Resent
26	Find good	□□□□□□	Find faults
27	Have high expectations of yourself	□□□□□□	Have high expectations of others

The Art of Self-Leadership

Inscribed on the tomb of an Anglican Bishop in Westminster Abbey, 1100 AD:

> When I was young and free and my imagination had no limits, I dreamed of changing the world. As I grew older and wiser, I discovered the world would not change, so I shortened my sights somewhat and decided to change only my country. But it, too, seemed immovable. As I grew into my twilight years, in one last desperate attempt, I settled for changing only my family, those closest to me, but alas, they would have none of it. And now, as I lie on my deathbed, I suddenly realize: If I had only changed myself first, then by example I would have changed my family. From their inspiration and encouragement, I would have then been able to better my country and, who knows, I may have even changed the world.

If you can't lead yourself, it is impossible to lead others! It's true. Look at the statistics from the Bureau of Labor Statistics:[1]

- Less than 20% of all people in the workforce today are in supervisory positions.

- Less than 5% are in executive positions.

- Approximately 2% are CEOs, church leaders, or small business owners.

- Only 1% of those who lead for-profit and not-for-profit entities in our nation are in the leadership position because they THINK like a leader and take calculated leadership risks!

Researchers estimate that at least half of the heads of entities rose to their leadership position on seniority, owing to the length of time they had been in the company, religious group, or business. Others assumed their leadership position as the result of a family inheritance or were appointed to the position by an outside entity in response to some form of success in a different and sometimes unrelated organization.

To a degree, these statistics are alarming. Most people know someone in an organization who achieved a leadership position through longevity, seniority, inheritance, or other means but who is not qualified to lead. The danger in this style of leadership is that there is no leadership, only people put in a place to make decisions affecting countless families without the proper skills and training to support their decisions. And unfortunately, many of these people at this critical level of leadership don't lead with excellence.

Look at the American economy today. The dumbing down of the American economic machine starts at the top echelon of leadership. But there is hope! And it starts with you!

I am a firm believer in people. And I am a firm believer in people leading with excellence from wherever they are in an organization. In his book *The 360° Leader,* my friend John Maxwell encourages people to lead from the middle. He states the middle of an organization is often the optimal place to practice, exercise, and extend your influence!

This has proven to be true in my life. It doesn't matter your position in life or in a company, you have the ability to influence and deliver excellence regardless. As you Discover, Develop, and Deploy your 1% Factor, you will make a difference wherever you are.

To be a leader doesn't mean you are the boss! It means you have the ability to lead. You can be a janitor, a CEO, a secretary, a

schoolteacher, a millwright, a car salesman—you can literally be
a person in any position, employed, self-employed,
unemployed—and still be a leader. It starts with YOU!

Leadership Is a Choice

*In the long run, we shape our lives and shape ourselves.
The process never ends until we die. And the choices
we make are ultimately our own responsibility.*
ELEANOR ROOSEVELT

Leadership is not about a particular position. Leadership is
about a choice—your ability to choose to lead yourself to be the
best YOU that you can be all the time. Leadership is a choice to
THINK, BE, DO to the best of your ability, all the time.

The discovery and recognition of your 1% Factor is a discovery
and recognition of your ability to lead. At a minimum, it is your
God-given ability to lead yourself. That's a big deal! People who
discover their 1% Factor begin to develop their uniqueness, and in
the process consistently become the best they can be all the time.

I have passionately studied Leadership for over thirty-five
years. But I have been striving to lead myself, in small and big
ways, for as long as I can remember. Recently, I was walking
through the airport and saw trash lying in the concourse in front
of me. People had stepped on, stepped over, stepped around this
trash, and it was still lying right there in the concourse. No one
was around—just me, the concourse, and a piece of trash. I
walked past the trash and headed to my gate when the voice in
my head spoke, "You just walked by a piece of trash!"

I said to the voice, "I have a plane to catch, and it's not my job to pick up someone else's trash," and I kept walking. Then the voice said, "It's not about the trash. It's about seeing something that needs to be taken care of and taking care of it. It's about seeing a problem and choosing to BE a solution. It's about order and taking responsibility to make any space you are in a better place."

I turned around, picked up the paper, and threw it away.

Next, a marching band came from around the corner. There were balloons, people were clapping, and all of a sudden, a man stepped forward and said, "Because you had the presence of mind to pick up that piece of trash when others walked on by, because you led yourself to do what others weren't willing to do, because you took responsibility to stop what you were doing that was about YOU and chose to BE the solution to a problem you saw, because you are the kind of person who doesn't care WHO gets the credit, it's my honor and privilege to present you this million-dollar check for your EXCELLENCE in LEADERSHIP!"

Obviously that did NOT happen. But let me ask you a question: If you knew it would, would you pick up the trash?

This is an example of why I say Leadership is a way of THINKING before anything else. The point is not about me doing some great deed. It is about being the best me by leading myself to do what needs to be done, *especially* when no one else is looking. It is about practicing the art of self-leadership.

Self-Discipline

The principle of leading oneself is called Self-Leadership. It is the ability and discipline to lead oneself, even in the most unlikely situations, and in my opinion, it is the highest form of leadership. Leading yourself with a mind-set of excellence by wanting

to be the best you can be builds self-respect, elevates your character, and improves confidence. As you increase in your ability to
lead yourself, you will have the confidence you need to deploy
your 1% in your world! Who knows? You may even find yourself
picking up trash in airports! Or better yet, leading yourself to
perform an act of kindness or service for another person you
would not have considered in the past.

Mindfulness

When my son was about eight years old, our family was spending a day at a popular theme park, and he expressed a need to
use the facilities. When we walked into the men's restroom, it
was a horrible sight. As I held my son's little hand, I explained to
him that this place was like this because people used it but did
not take the responsibility for how they left it.

Then, after using the facilities ourselves, we cleaned the entire
space up—to practice self-leadership. I wanted my son to know
that WE, the Crafts, take responsibility for making every place
WE are in a better place.

These stories are not about me, the trash, or cleaning public
restrooms. The stories are about finding a need and not just
filling it but also leading yourself to lead the need. It's about
being mindful of leading yourself in any and every situation you
choose, in a way that you can make a difference.

Your power to lead others is contingent on your passion to
lead yourself!

As you discover your 1% Factor, you will begin to build character and create inward trust because your unique greatness will
start to develop. It may start appearing in little things. And as you
recognize these little things, bigger challenges will present oppor-

tunities to develop greater depths of your uniqueness. Confidence builds internally, and there is a natural tendency to want to add value to others. Deployment is a natural extension of recognizing your 1% Factor, and outward action occurs.

Do Hard Things

The little things sometimes are the hardest things for us to do. But when you do hard things, you are training yourself to do GREAT things. When you take care of the little things, the big things will take care of themselves. It's being mindful of the little things that develops a spirit of excellence and sharpens your 1%. Any area of personal excellence organically develops your leadership capacity.

That is exactly why people can lead regardless of position in a company. And if executive managers can elevate their thinking to Discover, Develop, and Deploy their 1% Factor, their entire company will begin to achieve greater success. The same that is true for business is also true for families and individuals.

I am convinced and have proven through years of strategic process modeling that as you consistently lead yourself with excellence, others will recognize your greatness and follow you. You can choose who you follow, but you can't choose who follows you. Self-leadership will result in having followers. The reason for this is because you are giving the best part of yourself to others when you serve them. This was the secret of Jesus's leadership style—serving.

When you serve others, you create excellence that can be followed.

Servant Leadership: Your Gateway to Greatness

Leadership is born through the process of discovering that you have uniqueness about you that no one else has. You look at situations differently than most people. You long to make a difference. Slowly, that discovery leads to developing core values, refining skills, building character, and creating levels of trust. Confidence is gained through repetitive consistency. Then one day, an opportunity is before you, and you respond.

You have just moved into an elevated thinking process that is self-leadership. Self-leadership is NOT selfish leadership. It is not about being the best for your own benefit. Of course, you will benefit because you will create confidence, character, and trust in yourself. However, it is through serving others that your self-leadership develops to its fullest.

Leadership comes in many brands with a variety of labels. Serving others also has a name: Servant Leadership. Leading with excellence in serving others is deploying greatness, your 1% Factor, to benefit those around you. It is taking a step back so others can take a step forward. It is giving up your right to be right. I consider Servant Leadership to be the most noble of leadership brands.

Servant Leadership for Life (in Four Short Paragraphs)

Servant Leadership is a noble ascent of the mind and heart to live with a transcendent cause. It is born out of a grateful heart and expressed through a spirit of Generosity. Through Servant Leadership one's life becomes sacred despoilment of mediocrity.

Servant Leadership is an initiation of Greatness by the one serving and is intended to benefit the one being served. However, the real beneficiary of Servant Leadership is the one who leads by serving.

Servant Leadership is the most effective way to develop personal greatness that generates competence, attitude, and skills and empowers one to find a need and not just fill it but also lead it. By doing so, the one who leads himself to serve others, leads others by example and creates an atmosphere of excellence, where quality breeds excellence and excellence breeds quality.

Servant Leadership as a modus operandi develops the quality of indispensability that is the cause for all long-term growth and success both personally and professionally.

The greatest Servant Leader I know is my wife, Sheila. I have been the recipient of her Servant Leadership for more than thirty years; our three children are also beneficiaries. Sheila has a way of giving, and giving, and giving that seems endless and effortless, although I know she does, indeed, expend tremendous effort in helping and serving others. Sheila decided long ago to make Servant Leadership her mind-set.

Servant Leadership Is Generosity

Servant Leadership is first and foremost a way of THINKING. It is a perspective rooted in a person deciding how she wants to live, who she wants to be, and what she wants out of life. It is an ascent of mind and heart to live with a transcendent cause.

Most people do not live with a sense of transcendence. They live for today with little thought to their future. They are hoping that something good is going to happen, but they have no concept that they can help that good thing happen.

Servant Leadership becomes a way of BEING. A person becomes a Servant Leader in loving, in expressing faithfulness, in giving, in extending acts of mercy and kindness, in developing self-control. Servant Leadership is at the core of abiding peace and joy.

Servant Leadership is a way of DOING. It becomes both the what and the how of a person's behavior, not only at home or with friends but also on the job, in the community, riding the subway or driving the freeway, interacting with strangers, being a consumer or customer or patient or client—even walking the concourse of an airport. It is central to all aspects of leadership.

Servant Leadership is, in one word, Generosity. You are Generous when:

- You focus on what you have to give, not on what you want to receive.

> *Ask not what your country can do for you;*
> *ask what you can do for your country.*
> JOHN F. KENNEDY

- You focus on what is needed, not what you need.

> *Do all the good you can, by all the means*
> *you can, in all the ways you can, in all the places*
> *you can . . . as long as you can.*
> JOHN WESLEY

- You focus on what you can do, not what you can't do.

> I am only one, but I am one.
> I cannot do everything, but I can do
> something. And because I cannot
> do everything, I will not refuse to do s
> omething that I can do.
>
> HELEN KELLER

- You focus on helping others get what they want, rather than you getting what you want.

> If you can dream it,
> then you can achieve it.
> You will get all you want in life
> if you help enough other people
> get what they want.
>
> ZIG ZIGLAR

- You focus on bringing value rather than on needing to feel valuable.

> Try not to become a man
> of success, but rather try
> to become a man of value..
>
> ALBERT EINSTEIN

Serving to Lead

A man once shared with me his personal story of becoming a Servant Leader. He said:

> Early in my life and marriage, I have to admit that my life was all about me. I didn't particularly mean to be egocentric—I just was. My job was all about my work, my goals, my position, my advancement. My nonwork hours were spent doing what I wanted to do, whether working out at the gym or playing softball with my guy friends. My wife was pretty much home alone.
>
> Then I learned about Servant Leadership, and for the first time in my life, I made a decision that I was going to lead by serving. It was a 180-degree turnaround for me. The emphasis was on serving, not on being served, on giving more than on receiving, on extending myself toward others more than expecting others to put themselves out for me. Who benefited? Everybody! At work, at home, and at our church, including me.

Servant Leadership is not about being in the position of leader. It is about developing a disposition of serving. Leadership is a by-product of the serving.

I realize that such a perspective is completely opposite to what seems rational. In the traditional sense, leaders demand output and obedience. In Servant Leadership, a leader seeks to out-give everybody on his team. In so doing, he becomes the best leader possible in terms of morale, cooperation, respect, admiration, and loyalty. A leader who has the heart to serve so others benefit is worth following.

It is a fact that people are not equal in their talents and abilities, their intellects, or in any of a large number of other attributes, but everyone can lead themselves better. Even though we are 99% alike in our genetic makeup, we are far from 99% alike in our intellectual, emotional, spiritual, and physical CAPACITY. We can increase our leadership capacity by serving others more. We work at different rates, employ different skills, have different dreams, and have different personalities, propensities, and potential, but we can all become Servant Leaders.

We cannot guarantee equal results for all people or all efforts any more than we can place people into the same box when it comes to talent and ability. But what each person can do is: Discover, Develop, and Deploy (D-D-D) her 1%. There will always be people who are better than you at something, but they're not better at leading you than YOU are. There will always be people who are smarter than you on some level, but they don't have to be better at Servant-Leading than you are.

And there are always people who are born into privilege.

But NO ONE has your fingerprint! NO ONE holds the unique 1% you possess. NO ONE can D-D-D your 1% except YOU.

I encourage you with all my being to live up to YOUR God-given purpose that no one else has. You will never know the unlimited value that you bring until you D-D-D your 1%.

THINK, BE, DO

THINK: Discover

Are you more of a Leadership thinker or a Normalship thinker?

What part of your Normalship needs to be moved to Leadership?

What are some little things that you need to do now that are hard for you?

BE: Develop

In a word, what is Servant Leadership?

What do you need to be more Mindful about?

DO: Deploy

What part of Servant-Leading do you need to focus on most?

Who is the greatest Servant Leader you know? What makes him or her such a great leader?

What can you learn from your chosen greatest Servant Leaders and implement in Your 1% as a Servant Leader?

7

Your T-N-T

It's not what happens to you that matters most but what happens in you which ultimately determines what happens through you.

One of the greatest statements ever published, in my opinion, was made by comedic pundit Erma Bombeck, who wrote the essay "If I had my life to live over." She said, "When I stand before God at the end of my life, I would hope that I would not have a single bit of talent left, and could say, 'I used everything you gave me.'" I agree!

Randy Pausch published a thought-provoking book titled *The Last Lecture*. The book is a spin-off of a lecture he gave at Carnegie Mellon University titled, "Really Achieving Your Childhood Dreams." Pausch was a professor of computer science, human-computer interaction, and design at the university. His talk was modeled after an ongoing series of lectures in which top academics were asked to think deeply about what mattered to them and then to give a hypothetical final talk embodying the wisdom they would try to impart to the world if they knew it was their last chance to speak. A month before Pausch gave his lecture, he had been given word that the cancer in his pancreas, which had been diagnosed a year earlier, had reached the terminal stage.

In his lecture, Pausch told tales of his childhood, citing the important lessons he wanted his children to learn and encouraging his children to live life to its fullest—because you never know when it will be taken from you. I agree!

If Today Was the First Day . . .

Several months after I read Bombeck's essay, I wrote my own "If Today WAS the First Day of the Rest of My Life":

> *If today was the first day of the rest of my life, I would want to live with the wisdom of knowing what matters most.*

> *I would want to start with a clean slate, yet be consciously aware of the difference between good and great.*

> *I would want the people I care about to know, that is really all I care about.*

> *I would want to Discover, Develop, and Deploy passion with people and not ever be misunderstood.*

> *I would walk more strategically with a limp and be more aware of my strut.*

> *I would want to know what connects people deeply with God and seek to connect with them in God.*

> *I would want to speak healing words to mend broken hearts.*

I would want to inspire the best in every person.

*I would want my "I love you" to have more
impact than my "I'm sorry."*

*I would want to be fully alive in every moment
and be awed easily.*

*I would want to spend every day with the people I love
the most, giving and getting the most out of life.*

*If today was the first day of the rest of my life, I would
want to express that I love God, I love my family, and I am
grateful beyond words for GREAT FRIENDS. I would
give God my PRAISE for enabling and empowering
me to Think, Be, and Do what I love.*

And . . .

*I would find a way to make the past, both good and
not so good, work something in me to make me
more like Him whose image I bear.*

Choosing a Road Called Transformation

This poem, for me, is about how I want to live every day. It is less about giving and getting and more about Thinking, Being, and Doing. Robert Frost, the great American poet, wrote:

Two roads diverged in a wood, and I—

I took the one less traveled by,

And that has made all the difference.

I call that road Transformation.

Transformation is defined in my 1828 Webster's dictionary as a "metamorphosis: as from a caterpillar to a butterfly; a change of heart in man, by which his disposition and temper are conformed to the divine image." I must say, I love that! The D-D-D of Your 1% is your Transformational advantage.

M. Scott Peck, the author of *The Road Less Traveled*, wrote:

> The whole course of human history may depend on
> a change of heart in one solitary and even humble
> individual, for it is in the solitary mind and the soul of
> the individual that the battle between good and evil is
> waged and ultimately won or lost. The truth is that our
> finest moments are most likely to occur when we are
> feeling deeply uncomfortable, unhappy, or unfulfilled.
> For it is only in such moments, propelled by our
> discomfort, that we are likely to step out of our ruts and
> start searching for different ways or truer answers.

Often, something happens that forces us out of our comfort zone and makes us uncomfortable, and we end up focusing on that thing. We are unaware that it could become a defining moment. Unfortunately, most change for people occurs as a result of tragedy. Otherwise, for most people, there is no motivation for change.

Here's the challenge—to move from being transactional to becoming transformational! In life, we learn the importance of being transactional early. From the time you were a baby, people around you showed excitement when you achieved your first step and began to walk. It's what Pavlov taught with stimulus and response; we can become very stimulus and response motivated.

This is the essence of being Transactional, to live on the reactive side of life.

Transformational Leadership is not just about stimulus and response, but it is also about the power you have to make a choice between the stimulus and your response to it. The essence of being Transformational is to live on the proactive side of life. In this chapter, I want to not only teach you the difference between transactional and transformational but to also help you with your 1% to become more Transformational. I want to help you to become a Transformational Leader, not just a transactional person.

Transformational Leadership

In Chapter 6, "Your Leadership," I talked about what Leadership is and about how Self-Leadership and Servant Leadership are paramount to your 1% being realized. But now I want to emphasize what I believe is the more important kind of leadership. There are many styles and philosophies of leadership. But when you know what leadership is, and you align your Think, Be, Do with your definition of leadership, you are making great progress in the D-D-D of your 1%!

When you begin to master the art of self-leadership, you begin to understand thinking beyond normal and you then can know you have greatness to give others. As you mature as a leader, you will be motivated to serve others by becoming a Servant Leader. That is where leadership beyond yourself begins to bear fruit. You begin to understand that you can make a difference anywhere, anytime! When Servant-Leading becomes an instinctive part of your 1%, you become a Change Agent. You become a Transformational Leader.

Transformational Leaders . . .

- Don't just want to lead but also want to make a difference

- Live their Core Values everywhere, with everyone

- Live what they say and walk their talk

- Become examples of excellence for others to follow

- Are passionate about helping others fulfill their God-given potential

- Are willing to boldly grow where they have never grown before

- Are willing to see the unseen and believe the impossible, and inspire others to do the same

- Believe circumstances can change for the better

- Become the change they want to see

The T-N-T Difference

There is a difference between Transactional and Transformational Leadership. Both are involved in everything we do, but my goal is to help you learn the difference and lead yourself and others you influence to be more Transformational than Transactional. Based on our discussion in Chapter 6 about Leadership vs. Normalship, Transactional is more normalship in terms of a way of Thinking, Being, and Doing life and leadership. So in my view, there are many people who are in positions of leadership who are Transactional leaders because that is all they know. I make the distinction between Transactional and Transformational because your 1% being fully D-D-Ded is dependent upon you becoming more Transformational. Let's look at the differences.

Transactional leadership initiates relationships for the purpose of exchange, based on valued things. That's where most people are—they are not interested in the value of the relationship, just in the value of exchange based on things. This mindset and leadership style says, "It's about me, not about you." Some people spend their entire life being transactional—from their family to their career—and never know it.

Transformational leadership is initiating an engaging relationship based on interpersonal values that ultimately leads to a greater quality of life. In other words, you move to a place in your life where you are initiating and engaging in relationships based on the values that you have and the values that somebody else has.

Regardless of your position in life, or your position within a company, you have the capacity as a transformational leader to influence upwardly. It's not about the position—it's about the value you bring. In work, in marriage, in life, recognize that you are where you are for a higher purpose, a transcendent cause. You are there to bring your 1% and influence your atmosphere because you are governed by higher values. It's no longer about you; it's about the transcendent cause. The greater your transcendent cause is, the more transformational you will need to be.

Look at the list below and circle the words you most identify with. Be honest.

Transactional Leadership	Transformational Leadership
Skill	Creativity
Goals	Capacity
Performance	Growth
Rewards	Vision
Short-term	Long-term
Realistic / What is	Idealistic / What is possible
Objectives	Culture
Tasks	Transcendence
Results	Change
Efficient	Effective
Numbers based	Values based
Exposes pain	Exposes solutions
Positional	Exampsional*
Hireling	Servant
Organizational chart	Organizational structure
Techniques	Strategy
Product oriented	People oriented
Management driven	Leadership directed
Delegation	Empowerment
* Exampsional is a word I created that means "an example of how it is supposed to be."	

Look at the words you circled. Are you more aligned with Transactional Leadership or Transformational Leadership? If you're like most people, the highest percentage of words you circled is in the Transactional column. I am going to provide you examples of how to transition your alignment from a Transactional to a Transformational Leadership thought process.

Skill and Creativity

Skill is focused on what you can do and is Transactional. Creativity is focused on a better way and is Transformational. Do you know what happens to some people? They get so skillful, they lose their creativity. Sounds like a paradox, doesn't it? People get so focused on what they DO, they forget to BE creative, because they are not THINKING beyond normal. Our natural tendency is to THINK, BE, DO normal. Your 1% Factor is what adds super to your natural.

So let's change your paradigm. Put your hand on your forehead and repeat after me: "I'm going to change today." Now here's how you're going to change. What you bring to the table is not what you can do but a better way of doing what is needed.

So here's the change. Say, "Because I am always changing for the better, everything and everybody around me has a chance to change for the better too." Develop a philosophy that says, "Everything gets better when I get better." The creativity part begins with you figuring out how you can be better. Your marriage can be better, because you can be better. Your job can be better, because you can be better.

I remember that shortly after my wife and I were married, we were lying in bed one night, and I asked, "How can I be better in this relationship? I really want to be better." She lovingly looked at me and said, "You are great!" Later she confessed that it took her off guard (creativity) and she wished she had another chance! So about a month later, we were lying in bed and I said, "How can I be better?" She lovingly looked me in the eyes and said, "Well, since you asked . . ." She began to tell me ways that I could improve, from picking up my clothes, to helping her around the house since we both worked at that time outside the home. I got a pen and paper and wrote down what she said, and I made a decision to transform, to be better, and in the process, to make my marriage better.

Today, I still ask her the "How can I be better?" question. You know what is amazing? She began to ask me the same question back. As I began to get better, it made my wife want to be better. This is what Transformational Leadership is all about. It's not, "If you do this, I will do that." That's Transactional.

Goals and Capacity

Goals say, "Here's what I need to do!"

Capacity says, "I will develop my potential so I can be the best I can be in whatever I do."

Performance and Growth

Performance says, "How well did I do?" The focus is oftentimes as an individual contributor.

Growth says, "How well did we do, based on what was possible?" The focus is more on being a team player.

Rewards and Vision

Reward says, "What will I get if I do this?" and is based on what has been and what is.

Vision says, "I will give my best!" and is based on what is possible.

Short-Term and Long-Term

Short-term says, "Get the deal done at all costs!"

Long-term says, "Let's create a Win-Win for all involved."

Realistic and Idealistic

Realistic says, "IT is what IT is."

Idealistic says, "Let's make IT the best IT possible."

Objectives and Culture

Objectives say, "Here's what I want to accomplish . . ."

Culture says, "Here's what kind of atmosphere I want to create so I can sow and reap the future I want."

Transformational leadership is focused on culture. What is culture? Culture is the atmosphere that is created by certain attitudes, behaviors, and beliefs a group of people has. What kind of attitudes, behaviors, and beliefs do you have in your home? What kind of attitudes, behaviors, and beliefs can you influence in your company or on your team? Improving your attitude and changing your behavior is a part of elevating your 1% that will influence and impact the atmosphere at your home, at your work, and on your team.

Tasks and Transcendence

Tasks say, "I am focused on what I need to do right now." They are small-picture focused.

Transcendence says, "I am focused on everything because the thing is not about the thing, but every thing is about everything." It is big-picture focused.

Results and Change

Results say, "The end is all that matters."

Change says, "Between every beginning and ending, there is a middle. Everything in the middle looks like failure, but it's not if it brings about a good ending. The purpose of good endings is so there can be a new and better beginning."

Efficient and Effective

Efficient says, "Do things right."

Effective says, "Do the right things."

It is important to understand that both are important, but if you are not focused on Transformational Effectiveness, you can be efficient doing the wrong things! Jesus speaks about people who say, "We did good things in Your name, even miraculous things." He says to them, "You didn't do the right thing. You did good works, but you didn't get to know Me, nor did you desire to do My Father's will for your life. You thought about doing things right, but you didn't do the right thing. I want to have a relationship with you more than I want you to do things that you think are right that make you feel good about yourself. The right thing is to know Me and to do the will of My Father who sent Me."

Jesus goes on to say, "Whoever hears what I am saying and does it is like a wise person who built their house on a rock: rain storms happened that caused massive flooding. Tornado-like winds blew and beat against the house, but it didn't fall! The foundation was as solid as a rock. But everyone who hears what I am saying and does not do them is like a foolish man who built his house on a foundation of sand. When the rain and the floods came and the winds blew and beat on that house, it fell. And great was its fall" (Matt. 7:21–27).

The message is clear: In your life, you can work hard. You can make a good living. You can provide for your family. You can make sure they are clothed and all their physical needs are taken care of. This is Efficiency—doing things right. But if you do not lay a proper foundation in your own heart and life, you will transact your time, but you will not transform your world! Let me say it like this: your 1% is the foundation for the other 99% in your life.

Numbers Based and Values Based

Are you numbers based or values based? I understand most companies are numbers based. If you will transform to a values-based company, your numbers will increase. Value the people in the organization. Value the people and what they bring to the organization. Value your family members and what each member of the family brings to the family.

As we discussed in Chapter 5, live a Core Values–based life. It is one of the secrets of Discovering, Developing, and Deploying your 1% Factor. Numbers will increase, situations will improve, and you will build confidence in individuals, in the family, and in the organization, when you are values based.

Exposes Pain and Exposes Solutions

In sales, most people are trained to expose the pain, make it hurt more, then heal the pain with their solution. That, to me, is transactional. Instead, focus on relational selling, presenting a better, faster, more effective process; building relationships; and providing exampsional service. Build sincere relationships, and the products will sell in time.

Positional and Exampsional

Positional says, "Do what I say and not what I do."

Exampsional says, "Do what I do, the way I do it."

Whether in business, parenting, or any leadership role, Transformational Leaders lead by example. They never ask their followers to do something they are not doing themselves. Great parenting is not leading your kids by what you say because you are the parent-boss, but it is leading your children by example with the way you live. That makes them want to be the best they can be because they have seen you model the best you. You have the power to bring about Transformation if you live what you say and are the living epistle of your own philosophy. If you talk something you don't walk, no matter what your position is, you will fail as a leader.

Hireling and Servant

Hireling says, "I do what I am paid to do and no more."

Servant says, "What else needs to be done, and how can I serve you?"

Organizational Chart and Organizational Structure

An Organizational Chart shows who is in authority, and lines are drawn based on the chart. Organizational Structure is different because it focuses on people, values, and goals aligning. It is inside-out leadership, not top to bottom. It is the responsibility of each of us to take responsibility to bring about a positive change even when we don't have the authority to do it. In other words, each person in the organization, family, or marriage takes responsibility to make things better, not because they have a position of authority, but by giving their 1% to make things better. It can best be described like geese that fly in a V formation. They can go 71 percent farther by flying together than by flying alone. The lead goose thrusts his wings down and gives a lift to the goose behind him. The lead changes as the geese rotate from front to back, keeping each other strong by not depending on only one. If one falls out of formation, two always accompany him to help keep the structure strong.

Organizational Chart focuses on assignment. Organizational Structure focuses on alignment.

Techniques and Strategy

Techniques say, "What angle can I use?"

Strategy says, "What is my best and highest use in this situation?"

Product Oriented and People Oriented

Product oriented says, "What I sell is products, and the products matter most."

People oriented says, "What I sell is myself, and the people I sell to matter most."

Management Driven and Leadership Directed

Management driven says, "I oversee what you do to make sure it gets done the way I want it done."

Leadership directed says, "I will help you grow so that you can do what needs to be done, how it needs to be done, when it needs to be done."

Most people are familiar with management by objectives. This modus operandi is to give people a task to accomplish and make sure they do it. This is Transactional. A Leadership-directed person is focused on developing people and empowering them to do what they do best. This is Transformational. In business and families, I encourage empowering people so they can make a real difference. You do this by taking time to have a transformational interaction with them, not just a transactional relationship. This is a big, big deal and will make dramatic differences in your family and organization.

Delegation and Empowerment

Delegation says, "Here's your job. Now do what needs to be done."

Empowerment says, "I believe in you. You know what needs to happen. You've got what it takes to make this happen. What can I do to help you succeed?"

Transformational leadership happens when we encourage people around us to be the best they can be. It is one thing to tell people to do something because it is their job—that's transactional. It is yet another to see yourself as an encourager who inspires the greatness in others. You empower people when you encourage people. Anybody can tell anybody what to do. Anybody can be told what to do. But Transformational leaders empower others when they encourage people. And people are inspired to do what they can do when they are encouraged and not just told.

The Importance of Transformational Leadership

Why is Transformational Leadership so important? Because it is a way of Thinking, Being, and Doing that creates a capacity for the best things in life to happen in you and through you. You are operating in your 1% when you lead yourself IN CHANGE, by changing on the inside first; that gives you the power and capacity to help others do the same.

Studies show that followers of Transformational Leaders in a Transformational Culture are:

- Self-assured

- Content with meaningfulness in daily tasks

- Positive about their leaders and see them as dynamic

- Motivated

- High performers

Transformational leaders know to allow their greatness to come out anytime. They also understand there is great wisdom in knowing when to assert and when not to assert themselves for the benefit of the people who follow them. They know they do no one a favor by playing small. People who follow a transformational leader will perform at a higher level when the leader will lead by playing big.

You are surrounded by and infused with information. It is all around you. You have volumes of information inside of you. You have gifts and talents; you have experiences. Information will empower you. But it's up to you to process it, to develop it, and to find its highest and best use. The information you possess is up to you to maturate. Some people will never experience living a transformed life because they never mature the information they have.

As part of your D-D-D process, I want to encourage you to use the following Transformational Triad.

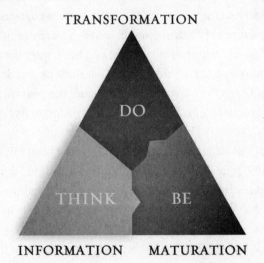

TRANSFORMATION

DO

THINK   BE

INFORMATION   MATURATION

THINK: Information

What information do you have? How are you processing or maturing it? The answers to these questions will determine whether transformation happens in your life.

Some people don't change until they've suffered enough that they want to, experienced enough that they learn to, or grown enough that they are able to.

Establish that today you want to learn and grow—to process information to maturation—so transformation happens in your life.

One way to THINK: Information is to Value what is Valuable. Think: *People over products, growth over sales, development over deployment,* and *alignment over assignment* for starters. I discussed in Chapter 4 the power of alignments over assignments.

Value all types of information. Establish a learning agenda in your life. Learn from the information you have, the information available to you, and the information that finds its way across your path. Learn from the good and the bad, the positive and the negative. Learn, process, mature the information to its highest value.

I was in the airport recently and overheard a man say, "You know what I believe?" He wasn't talking to me, but I stopped just to listen to his line of thinking. He continued, "I believe it was what it was and it is what it is." My first thought was, *That's where most people are today.*

But I would take it a step farther: What is possible in the future, based on what it was and based on what it is in your mind? You see, some people settle into it is what it is, like, *My marriage is what it is. My job is what it is.* There's no future, and they don't see any way to go to another level with this type of thinking.

What is possible for your future? I believe the D-D-D of your 1% is what makes anything possible for you. You see, it's not the smartest people who win. It's not the most talented people who win. People who make their dreams come true, whatever their dreams are, are not the smartest or the most talented, but they're the people who take information that's available to everybody, maturate it for themselves, and turn it into success in their lives.

No one can determine what you learn. Learn from everything. Remember these things about learning:

1. Your life lessons are your life lessons.

2. Learn from the mistakes of others.

3. What you learn is what you EARN.

BE: Maturation

Maturation is happening as you are reading this book. It literally means "the emergence of personal and behavioral competencies through growth." Life is not about what you are going through. It's about what you are growing through. In fact, you are going to go through stuff! I believe strongly that when you grow through what you go through, you create a BREAKTHROUGH!

Take the information you have learned, and the information you learn daily, and mature it. Process it. Determine what is valuable. How can you make the information work best for your benefit? How can the information you learned benefit others?

Transformational Confidence

You can gain Self-Confidence from the information to be a change agent. How can this best be accomplished? First, be willing to sacrifice anything in the present for something better in the future. If you are willing to do that, I promise you, you'll gain confidence. This can be as simple as saying no to fattening food because you want to lose weight. It can be as strategic as not buying something you want on credit because you don't want another payment. You build your self-confidence every time you decide to never allow the good to be robber of the best.

Just Say No!

Ask yourself, what is it right now I am willing to sacrifice for a better future? Write the answer down. Because the confidence that comes from that answer is: I know I could do that, but I choose NOT to do that.

Men, this is for you. According to the *Journal of Marital and Family Therapy*, 54 percent of men admit to having affairs and 74 percent say they would if they thought they would never get caught.[1] How does a man who sees a transactional opportunity (and that's what an affair is, a transactional opportunity) get on the transformational side of manhood? How does a man take that opportunity to build his confidence in being a man?

The Transactional thought is, *The affair would make me happy; I'd like that.* Men, it's an ego trip. It seems to tell you, "You still got it, and you can still conquer." Men and women, you have to realize the lure is a transactional lure. I know this is a deep, painful issue with some of you, but I want to give you insight on it, especially as a man.

The way you can build self-confidence is to know in your mind that you could, but you don't want to. You sacrifice whatever pleasure now for what's better in the future, and it builds your self-confidence. Most men, because they're transactional business people, are transactional relationally also, and that's why they make stupid, life-altering mistakes like having affairs. I address men with this because I am a man, and frankly, men do most of the affairing. I bring up affairs not to condemn anybody but to illustrate that the root of an affair is not just lust, but it also stems from a transactional mentality.

Great Relationships Require Great Work

Great relationships don't just happen. All great relationships start with you leading yourself to be a great person. Be the kind of person you want in your life! What kind of people do you want in your life? Be that great person. D-D-D your 1% so you can bring your 1% to every person and every situation in your life.

Now, women, how do you build self-confidence? Just know that in regard to your man having an affair, it's not about you. It's a deep wound for most women because it is a transactional, not a transformational, approach. So when you summon the courage to do what others won't, you will have in life what others don't. Being a woman of integrity takes courage. Refusing to live on the transactional side of life takes strength, commitment, and courage. Be courageous. You can have great relationships. To build confidence in yourself and your ability to have great relationships, you have to become:

- A Great Forgiver

- A Great Apologizer

Doing these two things will do more to build confidence in you than almost anything else. The most insecure people in the world are people who don't trust other people. It is very difficult to trust other people when you do not trust yourself. You are becoming Mature when you are working on being a Great Forgiver and a Great Apologizer!

DO: Transformation

How do you transform matured information into a leadership lifestyle? One way is to act on your confidence and build trust. You build trust by showing consistency in your confidence.

Confidence doesn't come because of what happens on the outside. It comes because of maturation of information. Confidence is the belief in one's own competency that empowers an assurance or firm belief in the integrity, stability, or veracity of another.

The way you see life is determined by the way you see yourself. The way you see yourself will determine the way you see others. The way to increase your confidence is to be people focused, to be change focused, to increase your personal capacity, and most important, to believe in your competency.

Build Trust

There are four ways to build trust. The first is to show consistency. People say, "Time tells"; I say, "Time reveals." Be consistent in your thoughts, your words, your deeds, and your actions.

The second way to build trust is to practice openness. People tend to be closed, guarded, and fearful. Fear is the enemy of great relationships, great achievement, and, most importantly, greatness that is born out of living with a Transcendent cause. Openness allows relationships to mature. The power of relationship is alignment, and with alignment comes opportunity.

Hidden within every undealt-with fear is undiscovered opportunity.

Other ways to build trust are to demonstrate your competence and to keep your word. Something as simple as saying you'll be somewhere at a particular time and then being thirty minutes late challenges not only your competence but also your word. Think about that. Being fashionably late is saying you can't be trusted in the little things—so how can you be trusted in the big things? Be a person of your word and bring the best of you wherever you are.

Your Life Story

Transformation is written by your life story. You are writing a life, a chapter each day, by deeds that you do and words that you say. People read what you write, whether faithless or true; what is life according to you? When people look at your life, it either influences them for the positive or influences them for the negative. Agree or disagree, it doesn't change the truth. Either you have a positive influence, a negative influence, or no influence.

You will develop yourself as a Transformational Leader based on your life story and the choices you make. Your life story will reveal if you were leading yourself or if you followed the crowd. So I encourage you to identify the key events in your life that brought about the most growth. Actually draw a timeline and mark within decades particular years when things happened that tell your life story.

Five Cs of Your Life

The five Cs of your life are: Character, Chemistry, Communication, Consistency, and Competency. Or, in more detail:

- Character—This is made up of the values that guide your life and displays itself in who you are when no one else is looking.

- Chemistry—This is your attitude and your Emotional Quotient as it relates to your relationships. It's your ability to create resonance, not dissonance.

- Communication—Ultimately, what you say about life, life will say about you.

- Consistency—This is doing what needs to be done, when it needs to be done, how it needs to be done, every time, because of who you are. When you have a history of being consistent, you can have the assurance of a better life.

- Competency—This displays itself in your sufficiency and efficiency—it's what you do.

In these five areas of your life, you are either going forward or you're going backward. They are sequential. They are chronological. Together they determine how you write your life story daily and how you build trust and transformational confidence.

The Anvils of Leadership

As you create your life story on a daily basis, you must learn how to capitalize on your anvils. What is an anvil? It's anything that happens in your life that helps shape you and brings about change. An anvil can be a test or a trial that challenges you to step up and be someone or do something you have never done before. Anvils can be used to lead to a new or altered sense of identity. Anvils help to define your 1%.

Capitalizing on your anvils requires using adversity, clarifying your values, confronting the normal, and developing finer distinctions (wisdom). There are two lessons in anvils. First, there is the lesson of leadership. Second, there is the lesson of learning about your hidden strengths and flaws. It's what you do with your anvils that determines your ultimate success.

There are three ways to capitalize on your anvils.

1. Create meaningful experiences.

Nelson Mandela was arrested in 1956 in South Africa for protesting apartheid. He had a four-year trial and in 1960 was found not guilty. The white judge was angry about this, so he sentenced him to five years in prison for being a protestor and causing problems for the government. His five-year sentence lasted twenty-seven years. In 1990 he was released from prison at the age of seventy-one.

Upon his release, he gave a speech in which he said these words: "If I had not been in prison, I would have not been able to achieve the most difficult task in life, and that is changing yourself."

He was in prison not because he did something wrong; he was in prison for trying to right a wrong. Did he create a meaningful experience from this injustice? Yes. He went on to transform the world in the process.

2. Increase your flex capacity.

No one can use what happens to you like you can.

The School of Hard Knocks is Adversity University,
where anyone can get an A.

One of my friends is a commercial builder. He has taught me that the taller the building, the more flex capacity it must have.

You increase your flex capacity in your body by stretching. Stretching forces more blood into the muscle or area that is going to be utilized. Similarly, you must intentionally stretch yourself in the areas of your life you wish to transform. Muscles that are not stretched tighten up and become pulled, making them ineffective. You can either stretch yourself or be pulled by others.

3. Neotenize your life.

Neoteny is defined as "the retention of youthful qualities by adults." So don't get old! Don't get crusty! Don't get fed up. Don't get irritable. Stay willing to take risks. Be hungry for knowledge and experience. Be eager to see what a new day brings. Get your childlike faith back!

> *Assuredly, I say to you, unless you are converted and become as little children, you will by no means enter the kingdom of heaven.*
> MATTHEW 18:3 (NKJV)

Moving from Transactional to Transformational is a life-changing adventure. Transformational Leadership will elevate every area of your life. Most importantly, as you lead yourself into personal transformation, what you learn will empower your 1% Factor. You will discover that if you can change and transform for the better, anything you are a part of can change. Transform for the better, and go from better to BEST!

THINK, BE, DO

THINK: Discover

Write out the character traits you want to embody in leaving a legacy to your family.

What is the change or paradigm shift you are willing to make?

In what three areas of your life can you move from transactional to transformational?

BE: Develop

What are some areas you need to mature?

What anvils have happened in your life that you can use to shape you?

DO: Deploy

Which of the five Cs do you need to work on the most?

Deploy your steps to move from transactional to transformational in the three areas you listed.

8

Your Life Sentences

*Your life sentences—the sum of what you
say in your life literally "sentences your life."*

I heard a story about Jim Carrey before he became a famous
actor, that he used to sit on Mulholland Drive, look out over the
city, stretch his arms out, and say, "Everybody wants to work
with me. I'm a really good actor. I have all kinds of great movie
offers." He told himself that there were all kinds of deals out
there for him. He would say these life sentences over and over
until he was convinced they were true. Then, the life sentences
became a reality.

It is the same way with you and me. When we envision what is
possible in our lives and put that into words and thoughts, those
words and thoughts create powerful messages that make real
changes take place in our lives. The things that we repeat over
and over are life sentences that set our lives on a particular course
and cause us to bring about in our life literally what we say.

Your Words Define Your Life

Life comes in Words . . .
Words become Sentences . . .
Sentences become Messages . . .

Messages become Experiences . . .
Experiences become Life Lessons . . .

Just because you have gone through a plethora of life
experiences does not qualify you to be Experienced.

If you do not learn from your Experiences . . .
You will create a culture of Crisis . . .

Crisis in any area of our lives is a
second opportunity to learn a Life Lesson . . .
If you do not learn from your crisis experiences in life . . .
You will Experience Chaos. The bad news about Chaos is . . .

It leads to Poverty.
If you choose to learn from your Experiences
You will create a culture of Opportunities . . .
You will Experience Order . . .
The good news about Order is . . .
It leads to Prosperity.

So in the end, the Words we choose to define our lives become
the Life Sentences that Sentence our lives . . . from Crisis to
Chaos to Poverty or from Opportunity to Order to Prosperity.

The Impact of Your Words

In Chapter 4, "Your Think, Be, Do," we discussed the importance of Elevated Thinking. I gave you the triad for Elevated Thinking and explained how to elevate your thinking so you can elevate your life. One of the ways I taught you to elevate your thinking was to construct your Words. In this chapter, "Your Life Sentences," you are going to learn why the construction of your words is so important.

Your Words Reflect Your Identity

Your words, to a very great extent, determine your identity in the world, and most certainly, your reputation. It's not what other people say about you that matters most. It's what YOU say! When you are saying the right words about yourself, the wrong words that someone says to you won't matter as much. In my travels as a motivational speaker and leadership strategist, I have shared the platform many times with Les Brown. I love his book, *Live Your Dreams,* which includes his *words* that have become his *sentences,* which have become his *message.* His *message* has created his *experiences,* which he has turned into his *life lessons* that he now shares with the world! My favorite quote of his says:

> *Never let someone's opinion become*
> *your reality. Never sacrifice who you are*
> *because someone else has a problem with it.*
> *Love who you are inside and out.*

One of my favorite books in the world is the Book of Proverbs. You find an amazing thing in the book of Proverbs: of the 915 verses/*sentences* of Proverbs, 222 (about a quarter) speak about this instrument called the tongue and the power of the words we use in our lives.

> *The tongue can bring death or life; those who love to talk will reap the consequences.*
> PROVERBS 18:21 (NLT)

Your Words Create Your Future

On January 9, 1969, Bruce Lee wrote himself a letter and used the words *My Definite Chief Aim* as the title. He wrote:

> I, Bruce Lee, will be the first highest paid Oriental super
> star in the United States. In return I will give the most
> exciting performances and render the best of quality in
> the capacity of an actor. Starting 1970 I will achieve world
> fame and from then onward till the end of 1980 I will
> have in my possession $10,000,000. I will live the way
> I please and achieve inner harmony and happiness.

By 1973, the classic film *Enter the Dragon* had helped Bruce Lee to achieve worldwide fame as an actor.

Your Words Influence Your Thinking

From the beginning of your life, words have influenced your thinking. Once you began to understand the meaning of words, you began to feel certain ways based on what people said to you, and you began to speak to yourself about yourself, which is called self-talk. Peak Performance Psychologist Denis Waitley estimates that our self-talk speed ranges between 450 and 1,200 words per minute. My friend Brian Tracy, a motivational speaker and author, says our think rate is about 550 words per minute. What that means is that we are speaking 480,000 words a day to ourselves!

The most important conversation you will have every day is with yourself because it cycles back into your own mind in the form of attitudes, opinions, and beliefs. There, your ideas and ideals are remolded to produce yet more sentences that develop, expand, or refine who you are. The cycle continues until you die. The ongoing cycles produce a positive or negative self-concept that you have of yourself as well as the impressions and influence you establish in the minds of others who hear you speak. What you say to and about yourself will ultimately determine what you say to and about others.

Your Words Can Change Your World

The spoken word has the capacity to ignite, inspire, and influence humanity for good or evil. The words we speak ultimately lead to crisis or opportunity, poverty or prosperity, chaos or order. Think about a few words that became sentences that changed the world:

"Give me liberty or give me death." Patrick Henry

"The annihilation of the Jewish race in Europe . . ." Adolf Hitler

"I have a dream . . ." Dr. Martin Luther King Jr.

"Mr. Gorbachev, tear down this wall!" Ronald Reagan

"Father, forgive them . . ." Jesus Christ

These are but a few of the people who have used their words to change the world. I could fill this book with quotes of famous people who are famous because of the words they spoke. I could recount speeches by history-making people who have said life sentences that have sentenced their lives, like Mother Teresa who said, "Christianity is giving," and her life sentence was to give herself away to the poor, lost, and dying. Nelson Mandela said, "An ideal for which I am prepared to die," and was sentenced to a life of imprisonment for twenty-seven years for the words he spoke and believed in.

But what about YOU?

Your Words Become Your Life Sentences

Let me ask you to complete the ten sentences below:

1. Don't try to reinvent the _____.

2. Be careful what you _____ for, because you just might get it.

3. Boys will be _____.

4. A leopard can't _____.

5. You can't teach an old dog _____.

6. Sometimes you can't see the forest _____.

7. Different strokes for _____.

8. I'm always sticking my foot _____.

9. Don't look a gift horse in _____.

10. Easier said than _____.

Did you come up with these responses: wheel, wish, boys, change its spots, new tricks, for the trees, different folks, in my mouth, the mouth, done?

I'm guessing you got ten for ten. Why do most people know these answers? These are just a few examples of life sentences we pick up along the way and unknowingly sentence our lives with the words we say.

True or False?

These statements are what I call life sentences in our culture. But are they true or false? Are they true for *you?* What happens when you repeat phrases like this in your own mind or voice them for your own two ears to pick up? You ingrain the Ideas behind these words into your thinking, and they sentence and shape your potential and character!

1. *Don't try to reinvent the wheel.* Doesn't that translate into, "Don't try to do something new"? Doesn't that sentiment translate into the idea that everything worthy to be invented has already been invented and there's not much you can do to make an old way better? Let me assure you, some wheels need to be reinvented. There's always a way to "build a better _____!"

2. *Be careful what you wish for, because you just might get it.* Doesn't this translate into, "Don't wish for too much"? And too much, of course, means more than you can handle. But who says so? What if you can handle something that's tremendously grand and fabulous and wonderful? Why not wish for it! Why not believe that if you shoot for the _____, and you miss it, you'll still land among the stars?

3. *Boys will be boys.* Isn't this just another way of saying that a certain amount of bad behavior can be expected from every person? Isn't this a way of justifying parenting by default rather than by design? And if your parents taught you that life sentence, didn't you believe that they were giving you an excuse to "sow some wild _____"?

4. *A leopard can't change its spots.* Does that mean that you are like Popeye the Sailor Man, who proudly proclaimed, "I yam what I _____"? Does that mean you can't change your character, or that you shouldn't attempt to influence another person's change of character? Are you stuck being you? Does it mean you should not expect—and reinforce—better and better character, even from someone who seems to have very bad character? Does it mean that God cannot transform the most entrenched sinner or redeem the most vile person?

5. *You can't teach an old dog new tricks.* Isn't that a way of reinforcing the idea that learning has a lid on it? Doesn't that mean that a person reaches an age, or a state in life, in which new habits can no longer be forged? What is it that you believe you are too old to learn, too set in your ways to change, or too frightened to try? Perhaps it's time to "take a leap of _____" and take on the new challenge!

6. *Sometimes you can't see the forest for the trees.* Doesn't that reinforce the idea that we often are so focused on the immediate and the temporary that we fail to see and pursue what is eternal and everlasting? Doesn't it mean that we have traded in what is highly valued for what seems critically urgent? Is it a matter of failing to recognize that "on a clear day, you can see _____"? Let me assure you, there is no

benefit to choosing to have limited vision, or in believing
that clear foresight is impossible.

7. *Different strokes for different folks.* Is that just another way of
justifying however a person wants to live as long as she is
supposedly not hurting anyone else? Isn't that a way of
saying we need to accept certain behaviors because we don't
want to speak out against them or "stand up for what is
_____"?

8. *I'm always sticking my foot in my mouth.* Isn't that a way of
saying that you never seem to know the right thing to say?
Well, why not? Are you just being careless, or are you
clueless? If you are careless, can't you begin to care enough
to "think before you _____"? If you are clueless, can't
you "get a _____"? There's no excuse for not trying to
get your foot out of your mouth!

9. *Don't look a gift horse in the mouth.* This particular life
sentence has been around since 400 AD. Saint Jerome
coined the phrase to refer to the practice of looking at a
horse's teeth to judge its age. If the horse is a gift, why care
how old it is? Use the horse as a workhorse or ride the horse
as long as you can! Jerome was a great writer, and he often
gave his writings away to people—no charge! People
criticized him for doing that. He replied, "Hey, don't look a
gift horse in the mouth," meaning, "I'm giving you the best
of me. Don't criticize it. Use what you can and throw the
rest away." It was a statement about gratitude—and it still is
a statement about valuing what comes to us without any
effort on our part. Be grateful for the good! Your mother
was right when she taught you to say please for what you
want, and "_____" for what you are given.

10. *Easier said than done.* Isn't this often voiced as an excuse for
    not making an attempt? Isn't this just a way of justifying
    our own lack of trying? Isn't this also a way of saying that
    "words are _____"? In truth, words are not cheap. As
    you have seen, Your Words are the most valuable things
    that you possess. Words are the ingredients of plans that
    shape HOW things might be done, they are the ingredients
    of explanations for WHY things should be done, and they
    are the bits that go together to make schedules and time-
    lines that tell us HOW and WHEN things should be done.
    The crafting of words related to deeds is often more diffi-
    cult than the deeds. But even so, is there benefit in using a
    phrase such as this? Why not say, "Let's roll up our
    _____ and get busy"?

I hope, of course, that you were able to fill in the second set of
blanks with these words: mousetrap, moon, oats, (y)am, faith,
forever, right, speak, clue, thank you, cheap, and sleeves.

My point in this little exercise is that the sentences we inter-
nalize become the messages by which we make choices and
decisions. Our choices and decisions relate to what we do and
experience. And our experiences over time become our life
lessons that lead us into order or chaos, opportunity or crisis,
success or failure.

Life Sentences Sentence Your Life

Since childhood, I have heard statements that have become all
too familiar in society. Most people are unaware of potential life
sentences in the midst of casual conversation and crisis. What
are you saying when things don't go right? The words we use to
define people, situations, and circumstances become life sen-

tences that sentence our lives from crisis to crisis or from opportunity to opportunity. Many people unknowingly disempower themselves by the life sentences they speak. But just as we disempower ourselves by what we say and what we hear other people say, we can also EMPOWER ourselves!

Let's look at some life sentences most of us can recognize and even complete without prompting. But let's don't stop at the negative. I want you to Empower your 1% by replacing old life sentences with new ones! Finish each statement if you know it (completed statements are at the end of the chapter):

Change: You will never amount to _____ .
To: I am who God says I am.

Change: I can't win for _____ .
To: God made me to WIN!

Change: If it's too good to be _____ , it probably is.
To: If it's too good to be true, God must have said it, and that makes it TRUE!

Change: I always get the short end _____ .
To: I always get the BEST because I am blessed and highly favored by God!

Change: I'll believe it when _____ .
To: I believe all things are possible with God.

Change: A day late and _____ .
To: I'm always right on time, and I have more than enough.

Change: I'm so low I have to _____ to see bottom.
To: I'm elevating my thinking so God can elevate my life.

Change: You always _____ .
To: You always make me want to be better.

Change: You don't love me _____ .
To: I am lovable because I am loving.

Change: If I didn't have bad luck _____ .
To: I don't believe in luck, but I believe in God's blessing.

Change: If it's not one thing _____ .
To: It's not about the last thing: the next thing is going to be my best thing.

Change: You can't squeeze blood _____ .
To: If you squeeze me, you are going to like what you find!

Change: The grass is always _____ .
To: The grass is always greener for those who are willing to plant seeds for where they want to go.

Change: I just can't keep my head _____ .
To: The higher the water gets, the more fun I'm going to have!

Change: Don't try to reinvent the _____ .
To: Build a better mousetrap.

Change: Be careful what you _____ for, because you just might get it.
To: Be intentional about what you wish for because you will get it.

Change: Boys will be _____ .
To: A boy's job is to become a man.

Change: A leopard can't _____ .
To: A leopard can't change its spots, but it can change its direction.

Change: Sometimes you can't see the forest _____ .
To: Small things in life are like trees; you have to put them in context so you can see the big forest.

Change: Different strokes for _____ .
To: Every person is different so that everybody can be better because of them.

Change: Don't look a gift horse in _____ .
To: The greatest gift you can give anyone is a healthy you.

Change: Easier said than _____ .
To: I will do hard things until hard things become easy things.

I want to encourage you to never again allow yourself to consciously or subconsciously say negative life sentences! Your Life Sentences are so important to your 1%! Take ownership of the words that come into your mind, the thoughts that are directed by those words, and most importantly, the words that become your Life Sentences! What differentiates you on any given day, in any given situation, is what comes out of your mouth.

Write down three negative Life Sentences that you have about yourself.

1. _____

2. _____

3. _____

Now, the most important thing is not those three negative sentences, but the fact that you can do something, right now, to override them. I just showed you how to change negative life sentences to positive life sentences! But there are a few things that I want you to further understand:

- Being positive is not a personality trait. It's not based on facts or feelings. It is a proactive choice.

- There is no positive power to change anything by being negative.

- A negative spirit focuses on negatives. A positive spirit focuses on positives.

Be Pro-sitive

You can develop your 1% right now by being PRO-SITIVE! You're probably thinking, *What is that?*

Being Pro-sitive is about being proactively positive. It's about being future focused. To be future focused, you have to be forward thinking. *Pro* in the Latin means "to be brave in moving forward." Being Pro-sitive is being brave enough to move forward in the midst of negative people, situations, and circumstances. The only reason people are negative is because of negative words and life sentences in the past that give them a negative view of the future. Be brave, look past the past, and speak proactive positive words, not reactive negative words. Be pro-sitive—the future is yours to seize!

Now write three pro-sitive Life Sentences about you and your Great Future!

1. _____

2. _____

3. _____

Sentences Become Messages

My son Josh came home one day from elementary school and said, "Dad, you'll never believe what happened today."

I momentarily feared for the worst. Then he said with a big smile, "Somebody called me a jerk."

I said, "Really?" Then I quickly added, "What did you think about that?"

He said, "Well, you know what *jerk* means, don't you?"

I had an answer, but I decided to do a little more investigating. I said, "Why don't you tell me?"

He said, "It means Junior Educated Rich Kid."

I said, "That's great, son! You are! And besides that, you are a man of God!"

He said, "I know."

I'm glad he knew. I'm glad he still knows. And I'm glad that he decided that no matter what the speaker might have had in mind in calling him a jerk, he chose to hear what HE had in his own mind!

Your Message Is Your Message

When people call my phone and I am not able to answer personally, they get my voicemail message:

> Thank you for calling! This is Keith Craft. If you are calling
> this number, you are one of the people I am believing
> the best for! Please leave your name and number, and I
> will call you back as soon as I can. Have a wonderfully
> well and blessed and highly favored day! God bless you!

We all give messages, leave messages, retrieve messages, and receive messages every day. From our phones we check our e-mail messages, Facebook messages, Twitter messages, and of course, our phone messages. Your tone of voice and ability to create resonance digitally and otherwise is more important than ever. But the most important thing you must realize in this social media–driven culture is: your message is your message.

You Are Your Message

Your message to yourself will determine every other message you give and receive. I have a ritual I do every morning that I have been doing since I was fifteen. Before my feet hit the floor, the first thing I do is say out loud:

> This is the day the Lord has made. I will rejoice
> and be glad in it. I can do all things through Christ
> who strengthens me. Good morning, Precious!

Why do I do this? Because this is my message to myself every day. These are the first life sentences of every day that are sentencing my life. So let's break it down:

> This is the day the Lord has made.

I say what God says about each day. I acknowledge not only that He made it but also that He made it for me! My message to God in this is that He is the Lord and supreme ruler of my life.

I will rejoice and be glad in it.

I choose to have an attitude of gratitude and pre-decide before anything happens that day that I will be glad, not mad, not sad, not reactive, but proactively positive—pro-sitive!

I can do all things through Christ who strengthens me.

I am speaking a life sentence right out of the Bible every morning. I am sentencing my life and clarifying my message that I am independently dependent upon Christ. I am saying, "He gives me the strength I need for the day, regardless of what comes my way." I am saying, "I CAN . . ." and in the process, my message is: "I am a CAN DO person!"

Good morning, Precious!

I am sentencing my life with what God says about me. If I believe I am precious to God, I have the power and confidence to make others feel precious! I am D-D-Ding my 1% by doing this so I can bring my best to the world, which God has given me to bring.

In the 1980s and early 1990s, I was speaking to public high school students forty-eight weeks a year. During that time, my message reached over nine million young people across America. I presented a message that we eventually condensed to statements on a T-shirt:

You are not who you think you are.

You are not who other people think you are.

You are not even who you think other people think you are.

You are who God says you are.

Please hear me on this. This is a life lesson you don't want to miss. For years in your life, words have created sentences that have become messages; messages have created experiences that have birthed life lessons. You have the power to reverse those life sentences and create new messages that become your unique experiences and, most importantly, become your life lessons. It's your choice.

Messages Become Experiences

The saying "You have to say what you hear so you can see what you say" is a simple truth. Begin to recognize the things you actually listen to in life and make the decision to put yourself into a place where you hear your words better, your sentences better, and your messages better. This is what makes spirituality so important. You can begin to hear what God is saying so that your faith (believing that God's way is better than your way) can produce a better life. The Bible says in Romans 10:17 that faith comes by hearing and hearing by the Word of God. As you read scripture, the message builds your faith. As you begin to say what you hear, you will begin to see what you say. What you say becomes the words, sentences, and messages that create experiences in your life.

When you speak, your ears hear what you are saying. Your Words set your future in motion. By speaking the power of scripture, you are creating life in your sentences. Your life sentences become your life messages that create your life experiences that become your life lessons.

The Greatest Message Ever Written

I believe that the greatest message ever written is found in the Bible—the Word of God. So if life comes in words, Jesus came as THE Word. The Word became Sentences; the sentences Jesus spoke, which were "re-spoken" by His disciples, became life sentences that can sentence our life for the good. But not only that, the life sentences also become messages that create our experiences as we apply the Word to our lives.

To confirm my point, the Bible in 2 Peter 1:1–4 (NLT) says:

> This letter is from Simon Peter, a slave and apostle of Jesus Christ. I am writing to you who share the same precious faith we have. This faith was given to you because of the justice and fairness of Jesus Christ, our God and Savior. May God give you more and more grace and peace as you grow in your knowledge of God and Jesus our Lord. By his divine power, God has given us everything we need for living a godly life. We have received all of this by coming to know him, the one who called us to himself by means of his marvelous glory and excellence. And because of his glory and excellence, he has given us great and precious promises. These are the promises that enable you to share his divine nature and escape the world's corruption caused by human desires.

As we look at this passage of scripture, we can see as we grow in our knowledge of the word and apply these sentences to our lives, the message to us is that it is God's power, which God has given to us. We have everything we need for living a godly life or experience. Our experience in sharing His divine nature creates life lessons in which we learn to escape the world's corruption caused by human desires.

Through His divine power, He has given you precious promises that only come through His word. If you understand the power of His word, the Bible, and that you have been invited to be a partaker in this divine nature, and you begin to speak the Words of the WORD, you will sentence your life to greatness!

Experiences Become Life Lessons

I am a voracious reader. Why? Because I believe readers are leaders and leaders are lifelong learners. I read to learn. I know what I know, and I know I don't know a lot of things, but I have a desire to know what I don't know, so I read. By reading all types of books from a variety of authors, I believe I am reading the very best that reading has to offer.

Some of the authors become mentors from a distance. These authors become valued for the information they share, and I am wiser for having read their books. Their WORDS make an impact on me in such a way that I implement new strategies in my life by saying what I hear from their books so I can see what I am saying in my life. I encourage you to read, even if it is only one book a month.

You didn't get to where you are overnight, and you aren't going to turn your life around overnight. But you can begin to see positive changes in your life immediately if you will begin to read and speak new life sentences. Remember, out of the abundance of the heart, the mouth speaks, so speak new life and a positive outcome into your future. I believe you will achieve greatness.

Re-Sentence Your Life

Life comes in words.

Believe.

Words become sentences.

Believe in God.

Believe in yourself.

Believe in others.

Sentences become messages.

It is impossible to practice Think, Be, Do in a way that is inconsistent with what you believe about yourself.

Messages become our experiences.

What you believe will determine what you will achieve.

Our experiences become our life lessons:

Lesson 1: The proof of what you believe will be evidenced by how you Think, Be, Do life.

Lesson 2: People will not believe in you if you don't believe in yourself.

Lesson 3: You will not believe in yourself if you do not live what you believe to be true.

Lesson 4: For you to achieve anything great, you must align your life with people who believe in you.

Life comes in words. Speaking positive words into your business, into your marriage, into your children, into your job, into your sphere and atmosphere will result in an elevated outcome. Here is a simple triad I recommend to guide you in the process.

THINK: Assess—As you Assess your thoughts, your words, your sentences, and your attitudes about various aspects of your life, you are Discovering foundational issues that keep you where you are in life.

BE: Address—As you Discover the foundational issues through your personal Assessment, you are more prepared to Address these thoughts, words, sentences, and attitudes by Developing new thoughts, new words, new sentences, and new attitudes to release the bonds holding you and to allow you to grow your 1% Factor.

DO: Progress—Progress yourself by Deploying your 1% through understanding the Discovery process of where you were and what kept you back, and implementing the new Development process to Deploy your greatness.

As you work through the Discover, Develop, Deploy with your thoughts, WORDS, and sentences, A-A-P your process to Discover, Develop, Deploy your 1% Factor, thus changing your life sentences to new life lessons that Elevate Your Thinking so you can Elevate Your Life.

The A-A-P process is something you can add to every area of your life. You can A-A-P your marriage, and I hope you would do that. You can A-A-P your job, your team, your family, and anything you want to be better. In the end, the A-A-P process is about what has been, what is, and what will be. In life, the most important thing for us to realize is we all have a past (what has been), we all have a present (what is), but the most important thing about your life is your future (what will be . . . what is possible).

So what is possible? I would tell you that whatever you say is what is possible for you to see in your future.

Completed Statements from Chapter

You will never amount to A HILL OF BEANS.

I can't win for LOSING.

If it's too good to be TRUE, it probably is.

I always get the short end OF THE STICK.

I'll believe it when I SEE IT.

A day late and A DOLLAR SHORT.

I'm so low I have to LOOK UP to see bottom.

You always SAY THAT.

You don't love me ANYMORE.

If I didn't have bad luck, I WOULD HAVE NO LUCK AT ALL.

If it's not one thing, IT'S ANOTHER.

You can't squeeze blood OUT OF A TURNIP.

The grass is always GREENER ON THE OTHER SIDE.

I just can't keep my head ABOVE WATER.

Don't try to reinvent the WHEEL.

Be careful what you WISH for, because you just might get it.

Boys will be BOYS.

A leopard can't CHANGE ITS SPOTS.

You can't see the forest FOR THE TREES.

Different strokes for DIFFERENT FOLKS.

Don't look a gift horse in THE MOUTH.

Easier said than DONE.

THINK, BE, DO

THINK: Discover

Discover and make a list of the negative life sentences you routinely speak over your life and replace it with a new, positive list of life sentences.

Discover and make a list of the negative life sentences you routinely speak about your family, your business, your marriage, your future, and replace it with a new, positive list of life sentences.

BE: Develop

As you Discover your new list of life sentences, Develop key words or triggers that will help you to speak these new positive life sentences instead of the negative WORDS.

DO: Deploy

Deploy your new WORDS and new life sentences to create new life lessons in your life. If you catch yourself making a negative life sentence, stop, correct, apologize, and restate it as a new life sentence. Ask for assistance. Recognize this is a lifelong process.

9

Your Winning Edge

Winning is habit. Unfortunately, so is losing.
—— VINCE LOMBARDI

"Just a second."

Have you ever used that phrase, meaning for people to just wait patiently and you'll be with them as soon as you can? Is this your way of asking people to hold on a bit, stop and breathe, and let you finish your statement? Are you delaying so you can wipe your hands or swallow your drink or do just one more thing first? "Just a second" sounds like a casual delay tactic.

What the vast majority of people don't realize is that just a short delay—faster than the snap of your fingers, less than one second—can be the difference between success and failure, or at the bare minimum, the difference between first and second place. Your 1% Factor is that difference to Winning at Life!

Consider what happened over a ten-year period of auto racing at Daytona and Indianapolis. Both the Daytona 500 and the Indianapolis 500 take approximately three to three and a half hours to complete. In a ten-year period, the winner who took the checkered flag won the race by an average margin of only 1.54

seconds. The winner took home $1,278,813 in first-place prize money, on average. The average prize for second place was $621,321, or less than half. What a difference a second and a half can make!

In the 2009 World Outdoor Championships Track and Field competition, a new world record was established for the 100-meter race by Usain Bolt of Jamaica. The new record of 9.58 seconds was 0.11 seconds faster than his old record of 9.69 set in 2008 at the Summer Olympics. Bolt also won the 200-meter race by posting a winning time of 19.19 seconds, only 0.11 seconds faster than his 2008 world record for the 200-meter of 19.30 seconds. David Rudisha of Kenya set a new world record for the 400 meter on August 22, 2010, with a winning time of 1:41.09, a margin of 0.02 seconds. One week later he set a new world record of 1:41.01, a margin of 0.08 seconds.

In track and field events and other athletic contests, special cameras have been developed solely to capture very small differences in time and performance. In a number of events and contests, the margin of victory between a gold medal and no medal, winning or losing, has been and continues to be judged by fractions.

In men's swimming at the 2009 Olympic Games, the difference between a gold medal and no medal was only 1.42 seconds in the 200-meter freestyle. For the women swimmers, the margin in that same distance was even narrower: 0.59 seconds.

In track and field, the difference between the gold medal in the men's 800-meter race and no medal was only 0.71 seconds; for women, the margin was 0.13 seconds. Truly, every second—or should I say every one-hundredth of a second—counts!

In the Summer Olympic Games held in Beijing, the whole world watched in awe as U.S. swimmer Michael Phelps out-touched a fellow competitor to win gold. The visual replays couldn't capture the difference. To the naked eye, it appeared that Phelps had either tied with or lost to the swimmer in an adjacent lane. But the highly sensitive touch pad device installed at the end of the pool gave the definitive result—Phelps had won the race by the narrowest of margins: one one-hundredth of a second. A blink of your eye takes longer than that.

What if Phelps had lost this particular race? He still would have had an amazing showing of six gold medals. But it was in winning seven gold medals that Phelps entered the stratosphere of superstardom in the history books—a position he just may hold for decades, or forever.

Consider your own life. What might have been the greater achievement if you had just spent a little more time perfecting a skill, practiced just a little longer each day, or given your performance just a little more effort?

Effort can be measured in a number of ways. Time is only one of them. Effort can also be measured in terms of output: mental, physical, and emotional. Effort can be measured in terms of focus. It is related to quality. It produces results. The core principle is this: winning requires effort.

Winning Requires Effort

Success is almost totally dependent upon drive and persistence. The extra energy required to make another effort or try another approach is the secret of winning.

DENIS WAITLEY

Nothing worth doing or having comes to us without our taking some degree of initiative or making some type of intentional act of receiving.

As a child, I was blessed with agility, speed, and athletic ability. I was fast, and I liked winning! I liked the idea of running across a finish line first. I learned from track and field events that there are two kinds of effort involved in winning. Some effort is displayed as immediate bursts of energy, very often in a crisis or crunch moment. Other effort involves sustained discipline, practice, and energy output over time. Most of us have experienced both kinds of effort.

A key principle connects these two types of effort: the more a person is engaged in a sustained effort, the more a person is capable of manifesting a successful and sudden burst of effort when it is needed.

Bursts of Effort

Bursts of effort often involve an immediate sense of crisis (perceived or real, it makes no difference). A person can and will run just as fast to escape from a coiled-up garden hose in the middle of a dark street, encountered while jogging after sunset, as he will to escape from a coiled-up snake. The burst of effort often involves a sense of panic that activates a fight-or-flight response, which results in an infusion of adrenalin. This produces added strength, which is temporary.

Sustained Effort

Sustained effort calls upon a different physiological system in the body—a system of measured and steady energy release. Two prerequisites are generally required: disciplined practice and body-mind coordination.

Disciplined practice is deliberately and diligently practicing to produce consistency in performance. Those things you consistently sow create the opportunity for a continual harvest. The purpose of practice is to become excellent.

Excellence is a way of practicing, according to your potential, as if at any time the game of life depends on your last shot.

I've missed more than 9,000 shots in my career. I've lost almost 300 games. 26 times, I've been trusted to take the game winning shot and missed. I've failed over and over and over again in my life. And that is why I succeed.

MICHAEL JORDAN

Winning at Life requires deliberate practice with excellence that is intentional and focused. It isn't just tossing the ball around or playing at the game. Deliberate practice is intended to develop specific skills through repetition. It involves basic drills, repeated running patterns, and twice-a-day workouts. Deliberate practice is periodic and rhythmic. Deliberate practice is aimed at winning, at excellence, and at greatness.

Body-Mind coordination results from diligent practice that involves the training of body and mind to work as one. It is practice that involves concentration, memorization, and ongoing discipline so that what has been ingrained through practice can be recalled quickly and easily, appearing almost effortless to the casual observer.

Over time, the mind-body coordination is finely tuned. The body responds instinctively to mental cues. The muscles required are already developed and strong, the perception is laser focused, and the routine is already established. Adaptations and variations are possible because the basic line of performance has been rehearsed to the point of being indelibly imprinted.

Winning Becomes Instinctive

The fact is that when you practice anything long and hard enough, you create an instinctive ability that becomes part of your 1%.

Not long ago I happened to notice something unusual about the keyboard of a person who is a superb typist. I noticed that at least half of the keys no longer had visible letters on them. I commented on this, and she said, "Really? I never noticed." The point: she never looks at the keyboard! She looks at her computer screen, where the words seem to appear magically and at lightning speed.

She said, "I don't even think about what my fingers are doing. In fact, if you asked me which keys to hit in order to produce a specific word, I'd really have to think about it and mentally rehearse typing the word in slow motion. The truth is, I can't tell you the order of the letters on the keyboard. I have been typing so long and so much that whatever I think just seems to flow through my fingers."

I want you to see the correlation between this person not having to look at the keyboard and your metaphorical finger-prints leaving an instinctive imprint everywhere you go!

That's the degree of fluency that deliberate and diligent practice can produce in your life through your 1%. Every top athlete knows what I'm talking about. The best golfers hit far more golf balls at the driving range and on practice putts than they ever hit during tournament play out on the courses. The best basketball players practice their shots at the free-throw line, the three-point line, and their favorite sweet spot on the courts by the hours, during the off-season as well as during the season between games. The best baseball players routinely visit the batting cages. The best swimmers spend long hours in the pool between swim meets. Name any sport you like, but more importantly, name anything in which there is a winner, and you'll find practice, practice, practice.

How to Win at Life

Winning at life involves Discovering, Developing, and Deploying your 1% Factor. I want to highlight four keys to Winning at life that I believe you should intentionally pursue every day.

Key #1: Practice, Practice, Practice!

Practicing is a critical component of the Discovering and Developing process to elevating your greatness. Practicing allows you to discover your gifts, talents, and attributes so you can focus on and Develop the areas of your life that elevate your passion, create your purpose to excel, generate a drive within you, and make you unstoppable.

Practice is the secret of the instinctive greatness of your 1%.

Some important questions to ask yourself are: Am I willing to practice what I want to win at until it becomes instinctive? Am I willing to do what it takes to achieve sustained excellence? Let me ask you:

- What are you practicing?

- How are you practicing?

- Why are you practicing?

10,000 Hours

One of the most profound revelations about practice that I have ever read was in the book *Outliers* by Malcolm Gladwell. The 10,000-Hour Rule in Chapter 2 was life changing for me. From Bill Joy to the Beatles to Bill Gates, Gladwell reveals what the magic number for true expertise in any field is: ten thousand hours!

Gladwell says that the thing that distinguishes one performer from another is how hard he works. That's it! And what's more, the people at the very top don't work somewhat harder or very much harder than everyone else. They work much, much harder.

Here is an excerpt from *Outliers: The Story of Success.*

> No one has yet found a case in which true world-
> class expertise was accomplished in less time. It
> seems that it takes the brain this long to assimilate
> all that it needs to know to achieve true mastery.

WOW! Could it be that practice is the key to Winning at Life? I believe with all my heart that it is.

Practice awakens the potential of your 1%.

The major golf tournaments in the world—the U.S. Open, the British Open, the PGA Championship, and the Masters—were analyzed over a twenty-five-year period (1980–2004). The average margin of victory for all these major tournaments was less than three strokes. That's less than a one-stroke difference per day per tournament!

I have absolutely no doubt that sustained effort in deliberate and diligent practice was behind those wins. Great golfers have years not only of practice but more specifically years of practice doing something they are gifted to do!

Practicing anything enough will produce improved results in that area. You are gifted and talented in areas that you will excel in with practice. Practice builds confidence. Inappropriate and inadequate practice yields frustration. If you want to be competitive in any area, you have to spend time practicing.

Five Things to Practice Every Day

Everybody should do at least two things each day that he hates to do, just for practice.

WILLIAM JAMES

Let me challenge you to practice at least five things every day. I can't tell you what specifically those tasks should be for you, but try to think categorically.

1. Practice Spiritually.

I call this practicing God's presence. Practice the spiritual part of your being. The most wonderful part of you is your spirit. Have you ever thought about why you are attracted to certain people and not attracted to others? It's more than physical. It's more than intellectual. It's more than emotional. What we are attracted to in other people is the same thing they are attracted to in us—the spirit of the person. As Pierre Teilhard de Chardin, the French philosopher said, "We are not human beings having a spiritual experience. We are spiritual beings having a human experience." (And for a short time, I might add.)

Allow me to encourage you to open your spirit to the Spirit of God. Read the Bible for yourself. Before you read it, ask God to speak His Word to you. Reading the Bible is just one way you can practice spirituality.

2. *Practice Emotionally.*

What I mean by this is to learn to rule your emotions. One of the best ways to practice emotionally is to practice forgiveness. You will have plenty of people in your life that will hurt you, and therefore, you will have more opportunities than you would ever want to practice forgiveness. Forgiveness is extending mercy when you are not required to do it!

Jesus was and is our greatest example of practicing forgiveness. He was nailed to a cross for the good He did and the bad we would do. On that cross, He said, "Forgive them, for they know not what they do." He practiced forgiveness on the cross in front of His accusers, scoffers, and executioners. One of the greatest ways both to stay healthy and to have great relationships is to be a great forgiver and a great apologizer!

3. *Practice Intellectually.*

I believe that readers are leaders. John F. Kennedy said, "Leadership and learning are indispensable to each other." Your ability to learn is one of life's greatest treasures because it will lead you to places you never thought you would go. I really do believe that being a lifelong learner is the greatest secret of lifelong success!

Practice Intellectually by reading books that inspire your thinking. Read books about key interest, finance, self-help, leadership, and other subjects that will expand your mind beyond your normal thought processes. I love what Albert Einstein said: "The mind that opens to a new idea never returns to its original size."

4. *Practice Physically.*

You have ONE body! That's it! The Bible calls it the "Temple of God." When you exercise, you are practicing physically so you can be healthy. God gave you your body to serve you, not for you to serve your body. If you bought a Ferrari, and it specified 93 or higher octane fuel, you would not put anything less in it. Why? Because of what you paid for the car. Its value and performance dictate what fuel you put in it and how you take care of it. The same is true of your body, which is worth way more than any car you could ever drive!

5. *Practice Financially.*

This is one of the most important things you can ever do for long-term success. When I was twenty-three, just out of college and newly married, my wife, Sheila, and I had our most important financial talk. I told her that I never wanted to live on more than 70 percent of our income. I wanted to give God the first 10 percent always, no matter what. I wanted to save 10 percent always, and I wanted to give over and above 10 percent. She agreed. We began to practice this in 1983, and more than thirty years later, we still live this way and have been abundantly blessed. My goal is to eventually do what James Cash Penney did: live on 10 percent and give away the other 90 percent—in my case, for the advancement of God's cause in the earth.

Generosity is one of the ways that you can practice financially and prosper for the rest of your life. I believe that when you are generous, you are the most like God—and the last time I checked, God has no needs!

As you recognize your 1% uniqueness, you will find that there are gifts, talents, and abilities that help you to naturally excel in certain areas. Discover them. Develop them through practice, optimization, and creativity. You will be encouraged, and your confidence will build. As you deploy your gifts, talents, and abilities, and begin serving others with your greatness, an elevated atmosphere will be realized, and you will receive a super-natural return. When you do this, you will be operating in your 1%. And you just might make a lot more money, have stronger friendships, and receive recognition you didn't expect!

Practice with excellence and motivation because it awakens the potential of your 1%! I believe you can win at life and achieve true success through practice. Practice with excellence. Practice with motivation. Practice refines your game and allows the greatness of your 1% Factor to be Discovered, Developed, and Deployed.

Key #2: Know the Difference Between Winners and Losers

In our politically correct (I would say incorrect) world, it seems wrong to call anybody a loser because we might make them feel bad about themselves. But the reality is that there are winners in life, and there are losers in life. One of the most important things you can do specifically in Developing and Deploying your 1% is to decide that you want to be a winner.

Winning and losing don't happen only in the sports world, where we see it on display and easily understand what it means. Winning and losing are everyday choices. Whether you realize it or not, everyone around you knows whether you are winning or losing. Most important, you know! Seek to know the difference between winning and losing so you can stay on the Win side of life.

Here's how to know the difference between winners and losers:

- Winners have Passion. Losers are always looking for passion.

- Winners have a Vision for what they want. Losers hope they will find something they like.

- Winners learn from their mistakes. Losers repeat the same mistakes.

- Winners look for ways to Grow. Losers see no need to grow.

- Winners fail and say, "There must be a better way!" Losers fail and quit.

- Winners think, "If it's hard, it must be worth it." Losers say, "If it's this hard, it must not be right."

- Winners see the end from the beginning. Losers see the end at the beginning.

- Winners focus on possibilities. Losers focus on obstacles.

- Winners are givers. Losers are takers.

- Winners are consistent in good things and develop good habits. Losers are consistent in bad things and develop bad habits.

- Winners do unto others as they would like others to do unto them. Losers do unto others before they can do it to them.

- Winners are committed to the success of others. Losers are out for themselves.

- Winners say, "You never fail until you stop trying." Losers say, "I tried once, failed, and I will never try that again."

- Winners find a way to Win. Losers find a way to lose.

You can probably come up with some of your own, but it is very important for you to understand that there are always Winners and Losers. The quote at the beginning of this chapter is actually a partial quote of a longer excerpt, which represents the Winning spirit of Vince Lombardi:

Winning is not a sometime thing; it's an all the time thing. You don't win once in a while, you don't do things right once in a while, you do them right all the time. Winning is habit. Unfortunately, so is losing.

Key #3: Be an Energy Producer

Winning at Life requires that you be an Energy Producer rather than an Energy Demander.

Energy Producers add value wherever they go.

Energy Demanders require that they be valued wherever they go.

Becoming an Energy Producer requires you to use the best part of you, which is your 1%. Winning at Life doesn't just happen. The choice to win is what puts a demand on you to be an Energy Producer as a part of your 1% Factor. Winning and losing are determined by Discovering, Developing, and Deploying your 1%.

I love the story in the Bible about the five loaves and the two fish. One day Jesus was teaching a group of people that numbered over five thousand. He had been with them all day, and as the day was coming to an end, Jesus said to His disciples, "We can't send these people home yet. They need something to eat. What do we have to feed them?"

Well, the disciples were very surprised that Jesus would suggest such a thing and said, "There is no way we can feed all these people! Even if we had two hundred denari (which was eight months' wages, or two hundred days of work), we could not feed all these people."

But one of Jesus's disciples, Andrew, said, "There is a boy here who has five loaves and two fish, but what is that among so many?"

Jesus said, "Bring it to me." So they brought it to Jesus, and after He blessed it, He miraculously fed more than five thousand people.

There are a lot of great things about this story, but the thing I want you to see is who the Energy Producer was in the crowd: the little unnamed boy! This story is not about the feeding of the five thousand as much as it is about the Energy Producer who contributed what he had so a miracle could take place! Energy Producers don't need a miracle because they are the miracle wherever they go!

Energy Producers are positive about people.

Energy Demanders are negative about people.

My friend Zig Ziglar said, "Some people find fault like there is a reward for it." Energy Demanders have a negative knack for finding fault. Maybe you had a wonderful Mamaw like I did, who reminded me often, "If you don't have something good to say about somebody, then just don't say it." I believe negative people negate themselves from greatness and from being the beneficiary of the greatness in others.

People who are positive about other people are not blind to their faults; they just know that to point out what Jesus called a speck in someone's eye, you have to move the plank from your own. In Matthew 7:1–2 (NIV), Jesus said, "Do not judge, or you too will be judged. For in the same way you judge others, you will be judged, and with the measure you use, it will be measured to you." Energy Producers practice proactive positivity on people, because they want that for themselves as well.

Energy Producers seek Peace.

Energy Demanders find Offense.

If you have ever been around someone who is offended, you know what it feels like to be around an Energy Demander. People who are offended want everyone around them to know they are offended. They not only want people to understand why they are offended but they demand that people take up their offense and be offended for them. I have discovered that nobody likes to be offended alone. Offense is a type of bait in a trap. By allowing yourself to get offended, you are taking the bait of your enemy, the devil, to entrap you in the dysfunction of unforgiveness. The problem with unforgiveness is that it leads to bitterness. Once you become bitter about one person or thing, your spirit begins to be bitter. The Bible says in Hebrews 12:14–15 (NKJV), "Pursue peace with all people, and holiness, without which no one will see the Lord: looking carefully lest anyone fall short of the grace of God; lest any root of bitterness springing up cause trouble, and by this many become defiled." The divine antidote for offense is forgiveness!

Energy Producers bring their 1% into every sphere.

Energy Demanders bring their fear into every sphere.

As you have learned, as you D-D-D your 1% and you use your fingerprint that nobody else has to leave an imprint that nobody else can leave, you are gaining the capacity to elevate every atmosphere that you enter. But think about the opposite. If you are insecure, if you doubt yourself, if you don't know what you bring, what are you bringing everywhere you go? You're bringing your fear into every sphere. When you feel insecure, you feel insignificant. When you are operating in your 1%, you will feel significant. You will know that whatever room you are in, you can make a difference if you choose to. The quickest way to feel significant is to take action.

*Our deepest fear is not that we are inadequate.
Our deepest fear is that we are powerful beyond
measure. It is our light, not our darkness, that
most frightens us. We ask ourselves, who am I to
be brilliant, gorgeous, talented, fabulous? Actually,
who are you not to be? You are a child of God.
Your playing small doesn't serve the world. There's
nothing enlightened about shrinking so that
other people won't feel insecure around you. We are
all meant to shine, as children do. We were born
to make manifest the glory of God that is within
us. It's not just in some of us; it's in everyone. And
as we let our own light shine, we unconsciously
give other people permission to do the same. As
we're liberated from our own fear, our presence
automatically liberates others.*

MARIANNE WILLIAMSON

Characteristics of an Energy Producer

- Generous

- Merciful

- Grateful

- Forgiving

- Apologetic

- Enthusiastic

- Positive

- Encouraging

- Friendly

- Hope giving

- Serving

- Defending

- Believing

- Emotionally healthy

- Resilient

- Solution focused

- Fighting for the best

Key #4: Be All In

If you are in a friendship, be All In. If you are in a job, be All In. If you are in a church, be All In. Whatever you are in deserves your All In!

If you're All In, your life proves it in all areas of your life. What proof do you have of being All In? If you leave, back down, don't take a stand; if you cover yourself without covering others; if you make it about *me* and not *we,* you're NOT All In.

Leaders who are truly All In are consistent in who they are—no matter what! They are persistent in what they stand for and WHO they stand for and, yes, time does tell. They become Omnipotent Warriors who fight against the darkness of mediocrity, insecurity, and normal thinking, being, and doing!

Are You All In?

All In: What does it mean?

Two small words, but they are essential to a dream.

You can talk All In or you can BE All In,

But one thing is for sure, there's only one way you can win.

All In is more than theoretical.

You can talk it; you can say it and even sound poetical.

But All In means, just what it means.

Being All In makes a dream, THE dream.

You can't be All In and be by yourself.

It takes more than you to get a dream off the shelf.

You have to have people whom you invest yourself in.

You see you're not All In without people: you need people to win.

All In is about you being the best you that you can be.

It's not about you if it's "what's in it for me?"

It's about sacrificing what you thought "it" would be.

By being All In, you discover your true Me!

All In will awaken the strong and reveal the weak.

It will introduce you to yourself, what you're not, and what you seek.

Until you are All In, you will never know the depth

Of what you have in you, that you didn't know you had left.

All In is a commitment to go where you've never been.

It's about the right people in the right places
doing the right things to win.

All In: What does it mean?

It's doing whatever it takes to make a dream . . . THE dream!

THINK, BE, DO

THINK: Discover

What are you practicing to win in your marriage? On the job? In your business? In your relationships?

What are you Discovering that produces energy in your marriage? On the job? In your business? In your relationships?

BE: Develop

From the Five Things to Practice Every Day list, what do you need to practice more to give you more of a winning edge?

How can you Develop yourself to be more of an Energy Producer?

DO: Deploy

What are the strategies you need to Deploy to produce energy in your marriage? On the job? In your business? In your relationships?

How are you going to Deploy your 1% through Practice Winning? In Servant Leadership? As an Energy Producer?

10

Your Blind Spots

Blind Spots are the parts of you that you don't see
That are keeping you from being all that you can be.

A man had a parrot that was loud and rude. The parrot spent all day long on his perch, calling his owner names and using profanity.

One day, the owner had had enough. He grabbed the parrot by the neck and shoved him into the freezer. The owner heard the bird yelling more profanity from inside the freezer. Then, suddenly, everything went silent.

After a few minutes, the owner worried that he had actually hurt the parrot. He opened the freezer door and pulled the bird back out.

"I would like to apologize," said the parrot. "I have used language that was totally uncalled for, and there was no reason for me to talk to you that way. I'm sorry." Then he said, "By the way, what did the turkey do?"

We all, like the parrot, have moments when we have to take a step back and look at what we're doing. In my case, the first time I realized this was when I went to a friend's house for dinner. I was a teenager, and my parents had taught me discipline and responsibility from an early age.

I was taught to make my bed as soon as I got out of it. I was taught that clothes belonged in closets and drawers, not on chairs and floors. I was taught to clean up after myself, and to keep my room clean and my possessions in good order. I grew up knowing how to wash and dry dishes, dust and vacuum, and brush and floss.

Frankly, I never questioned whether my mother was being unreasonable or wise. I just accepted life as it was in the Craft household—we were required to be clean, neat, self-responsible people who respected other people and their property.

My "I Can Help" Blind Spot

And it was with this perspective indelibly etched into my mind that I went to a friend's house for dinner. I noticed as I entered the kitchen that the top of the refrigerator was very dusty. I thought, *They can't see this dust. But I'm six-foot-six, and I can see it. They can't reach to the top of the refrigerator, but I can!* So I said, "I would be glad to clean off the top of your refrigerator. It is really dusty. Do you have a rag I could use?"

My friend's mother said a quiet little "Okay," and let me get on with the business of being Mr. Clean.

Then, as we sat down to dinner at the dining table, I noticed that the light fixture above the dining table had trapped a significant amount of debris, and even a few bugs to go with the dirt. I said, "Hey, I can see your light fixture also needs to be cleaned. Let me do that for you right now!" I assumed, once again, that the light fixture was dirty simply because the residents of that house were short.

Again, my friend's mother said in a quiet little voice, "Okay." I proceeded to unscrew the light fixture and clean it even though we hadn't finished eating at the table just below the fixture! It was dusty and filled with little bug remains. In retrospect, I don't think any of that debris fell into the food.

From my perspective, I was being a helpful friend, uniquely gifted by my height to resolve an immediate need. From my perspective, my behavior was value-free; I made no judgments about either my friend or his parents.

From their perspective . . . well, who knows? We never discussed it. But when I shared what had happened, and how helpful I had been, with someone who wasn't there for dinner, my glaring blind spot came into clear focus!

"You did what? How could you have done that, Keith? Don't you know how rude that was? Those people will never invite you into their home again! You could lose a good friendship!"

I was stunned, but I realized in a profound learning moment that I had not been the most gracious of guests. I discovered out of that experience that I had a serious blind spot when it came to the appropriate ways to offer help to other people. I also learned that I simply didn't know a very basic truth about families as a whole: not all families have the same standards set by my mother.

Paradigms Breed Blind Spots

Your paradigms are the breeding ground for most of your blind spots. The term *paradigms* refers to accepted examples of practice. Paradigms are the way we perceive, think, and value the world based upon a particular vision of reality. They provide us with a valid set of expectations about what will probably occur based upon a shared set of assumptions.

Paradigms establish boundaries and define how to succeed or fail within the boundaries. When we are in the middle of a paradigm, it is difficult to imagine any other paradigm. Thus, a blind spot! Conditions are ripe for a paradigm shift when a person or a number of people agree that the old ways no longer solve important problems or produce the results that are wanted. One of my purposes in writing this book is to awaken your 1% and disturb your present paradigm so that your blind spots are disempowered from making you UNSTOPPABLE!

Blind spots are part of our 99% similarity. Every person has blind spots when it comes to his own behavior, character, and personal worth. To complicate matters, your blind spots aren't my blind spots—and mine are not yours. We see the blind spots of others, even though we rarely see our own. When you begin to deal with your blind spots, you are successfully engaging and energizing your 1%.

Blind Spots Defined

So just what is a blind spot? A *blind spot* is defined as "a portion of a field of view that cannot be seen or inspected with available equipment; or an area in which one fails to exercise judgment or discrimination." For instance, you are driving your vehicle down the road and notice a slow-moving truck a few hundred yards ahead. You put your blinker on to change lanes, look quickly in your mirrors, and begin to steer your vehicle into the next lane when a loud horn forces you back into your lane.

You looked in the mirrors and didn't see anything. The vehicle attached to the loud horn was in the blind spot of the mirrors. To see into the blind spot, you would need to look in your mirror and then quickly turn your head to see what is outside your mirror's field of view.

Ecliptic Solutions

- In life, blind spots are often obvious to others, but we are oblivious to them.

- Ecliptic Solution: Invite people who know you to honestly share with you what they may see as potential blind spots.

- Blind spots are parts of our paradigm that we think are perfectly acceptable, yet our actions do not produce energy in others, causing more harm than good. Therefore, any influence we could have in other people's lives is hindered by something perceived as a weakness by others.

- Ecliptic Solution: Constantly evaluate your strengths and measure your personal effectiveness by whether or not you are an Energy Producer or an Energy Demander.

- Blind spots are things we consider to be truthful but are actually truth-fool because we have bought into something that is not actually truth but is just what we believe to be true.

- Ecliptic Solution: Pursue love-based truth by choosing to believe the best in others first.

- Blind spots are invisible areas of our lives that build invisible walls around us, causing visible success or outcomes to elude us.

- Ecliptic Solution: Identify areas of insecurity and become tenaciously intolerant with them within yourself.

- Blind spots are delusions born out of a desire to live with minimal pain and discomfort.

- Ecliptic Solution: Learn to embrace pain that causes gain, and be willing to get out of your comfort zone.

You Can't See Past the End of Your Nose

One day while driving, I was listening to talk radio. The radio station was doing a live call-in show about first-date experiences. It was hilarious, but there was one particular caller who got my attention:

CALLER: *I was listening to your show and wanted to call in and tell you about a recent first date I had that I will never forget!*

RADIO HOSTESS: *Please do tell!*

CALLER: *One of my friends had me set up on a blind date with this girl. He said, "You've got to meet her! She is incredibly beautiful. She's smart, she's funny, and I think you guys would have a great time." We set the date and when I picked her up, I could not believe how gorgeous she was, and it seemed that we had immediate chemistry.*

RADIO HOSTESS: *Did she seem to like you?*

CALLER: *Oh, yeah! We hit it off immediately!*

RADIO HOSTESS: *Well, tell us what happened!*

CALLER: *We go to this great restaurant. The atmosphere was perfect. The food was fantastic. We are having a great time when it happened.*

RADIO HOSTESS: *What? Tell us!*

CALLER: *This gorgeous woman looks across the table at me and says, "Can I ask you something?" I said, "Sure! Anything!" She said,*

"You are a good-looking guy. I'm having a great time with you, but I have to ask you . . ." "What?" I said, "Anything!" She said, "I just feel like I can tell you that your nose hair is distracting. You're so good-looking, and if you would just trim those nose hairs, you would be perfect!"

RADIO HOSTESS: *What did you say?*

CALLER: *Well, not much, but at that point, I decided the date was over and couldn't wait to get her home. I couldn't believe she said that!*

RADIO HOSTESS: *Can I ask you a question?*

CALLER: *Sure!*

RADIO HOSTESS: *Did you cut the nose hair?*

CALLER: *I sure did!*

RADIO HOSTESS: *You better go find that girl and marry her!*

The idiom, "You can't see past the end of your nose!" means that you think so much about yourself and what affects you that you do not see what is really important. The caller could not see that his nose hairs were a distraction. He literally had a blind spot at the end of his nose. When the girl pointed out his blind spot, he was so offended by what she said that he could not see the benefit of having someone like her in his life. The interesting thing is that despite being offended, he took her advice!

I believe the effectiveness of your 1% Factor will be dependent on how you deal with your blind spots. Your blind spots are your ways of thinking, being, and doing that become limiting factors and make you stoppable rather than UNSTOPPABLE! So the goal of this chapter is to help you SEE more, and therefore Be more effective. To be more effective requires you to discover your blind spots, develop long-lasting solutions to prevent your blind spots from being detractors in your life, and deploy your excellence.

How to See More So You Can Be More

In order to SEE more so you can BE more:

- See more of how your long-held habits are keeping you from Being in your present condition and situation.

- Focus more on what you are Being with your heart than what others are doing with their hands.

- See more of how to Honor, so you won't Be ineffective.

- Make your relationships more about giving honor where, when, how, and to whom you can rather than about what you can get.

- See more with Understanding, so you can Be less offendable.

Psalms 119:165 (NIV) says, "Great peace have those who love Your law, and nothing can make them stumble." Remember:

- Measurable success in one thing breeds overconfidence and the need to be right. But what's important is not being right—what's important is being open to learning.

- See more beyond the natural so you can be more super-natural.

- Expand beyond your understanding so you are standing on more than what is under your standing.

Blind Spots Are a Form of Insanity

The vast majority of people seem to think what they are doing is acceptable, even if everybody around them sees their behavior as injurious, inappropriate, or rude. They appear to think they are better or worse than they truly are. Most people think they are living in a way that is going to produce a better future than their past, even though they are doing nothing to change their habits, set goals for their future, or move past their failures. We must never forget that one of the defining marks of insanity is repeating bad behavior that produced bad results, and hoping that the next time we engage in that bad behavior, we are going to get good results!

Albert Einstein said, "Insanity is doing the same thing over and over again and expecting different results." If you aren't discovering and developing your 1% Factor, could you be engaging in insanity?

The vast majority of people go through life making adjustments according to circumstances rather than what they want for an outcome. They are living blindly, in what I call default. They give little thought to future consequences. They spend little time analyzing their associations or reevaluating their own beliefs and opinions. In simple terms, there are people who don't know what they don't know. I refuse to live that way.

The bad part about a blind spot is that it is a BLIND spot. You can't see what you don't see! Even more of a disaster, however, is the fact that few people attempt to compensate for their blind spots, even though they intuitively know that blind spots exist.

The first effort we must make, therefore, is an effort to see. We must admit to ourselves that we have blind spots and then seek to discover what they are. Only then can we begin to navigate through life with fewer calamities and greater success.

Good NEWS

I have an approach toward dealing with blind spots that I call the NEWS approach. NEWS stands for North, East, West, and South, like the four directional points on a compass. I use NEWS as an acronym for a different set of words.

N Is for Nirvana

Let me assure you that *nirvana* is not a term that originated with Buddhism, Jainism, or Hinduism. The word has become popular in Buddhist circles, but the word itself has value and meaning apart from Buddhism. *Nirvana* means "a state of freedom and joy that is not bound by pain or worry." It is a state that is not impacted by any factors from the external world.

Nirvana is the capacity to feel joy in the midst of a very difficult situation. Nirvana is the ability to feel peace even in the midst of chaos. Nirvana is feeling confident and secure even in a world that is in tremendous flux. It is feeling hope that you can't attribute to external forces. Nirvana is having faith that is rooted in what you believe, not what you see.

Nirvana asks the question, what is possible? I bring that question back to the originator of all true possibilities; I ask, what does God say is possible?

If God says the BEST is possible, then I'm going to run as fast as I can toward the BEST. If God says MORE is possible, then I'm going to go for more. If God says that WHOLENESS is His plan, then I'm going to do whatever I can to pursue wholeness. If God says that His SUPER can be added to my natural, then I want to be super-natural!

Blind spots in our lives often develop because we have closed our eyes, and our hearts, to possibility. We see only the looming giants of impossibility. We concern ourselves with what can't be done, what shouldn't be tried, what won't work, and what may not happen.

If you believe something CAN happen, it has a far greater likelihood of happening. If you believe something WILL happen, you will act accordingly and prepare for it to come to pass. Henry Ford said, "Whether you think that you can, or that you can't, you are usually right." I have proven that an elevated thought process, when appropriate action follows, can and will produce results.

My encouragement to you is to believe that a greater GOOD can happen, that something better WILL happen, and that you can use your personal faith, influence, and effort to make every good possibility a reality.

E Is for Experience

Experience leads us to an understanding of what was. What worked in the past? Is it working now? If so, how can we retain what works? If not, how can we revive what worked? What traditions were once in place? Why were they discarded? Why were those traditions established in the first place? Have we devalued some things that still have value?

The fact is that just because you have gone through a plethora of life experiences does not mean you are experienced. You benefit from and become experienced when you learn from both your own experiences and the experiences of others.

As you look back over your own life, or your marriage or company, you likely will recognize some things that you wish had never happened. And those are things that you need to Assess, Address, and Progress occasionally so they never happen again. You likely will recognize some things that you wish still happened, and you are likely wise to ask why those things have disappeared from your life and what you might do to regain them.

A friend said to me not long ago, "I stand in awe of my parents. Somehow Mom made dinner from scratch every night using a regular stovetop or oven. Dad went to our ball game

practices, and we kids were in bed each night by eight o'clock.
Mom and Dad made it to bed by ten.

"What happened? I can barely get food cooked in a microwave.
Each person in the family has to eat at different times. My husband doesn't get home until the kids are in their pajamas. And
even if the children are in bed by nine o'clock, which we think is
doing pretty good, my husband and I never seem to turn out the
lights until well after midnight. And more than that; my mother
didn't work outside the home. My husband and I both work full
time, and we can hardly make ends meet. What happened?"

I encouraged her to explore her concerns and questions.
There's a blind spot there, and it's a blind spot for our entire
culture! How did we get so busy? How did we get to the place of
needing so much instant gratification? How did we become so
bent on acquiring what is temporary rather than intent on
building what lasts?

There are many people who do not believe the Holocaust
really happened. They think it is movie stuff, based on fiction
more than fact. Are these people blind to what WAS?

I also read not long ago that surveys are showing people to be
nearly as prejudiced racially as they were fifty years ago! Are
people blind to what WAS?

It is an old axiom that those who fail to study history repeat its
worst moments. This is true not only on a global or national
scale but also on a personal level. Does the person who has been
through a divorce understand what really happened? Has she
learned and grown so that a future marriage can succeed? Does
the person who survived a heart attack understand how to regain
and retain a healthy heart? Has he changed basic lifestyle
patterns in a lasting way? Does the person who went through
bankruptcy know how to manage future income and invest-
ments? Has she learned what not to do as well as what to do?

We must have a good understanding of our own experience if we are going to overcome our blind spots. We must know and learn from what was, or blind spots are going to proliferate!

W Is for Wisdom

Wisdom asks the question, what is best?

Many things in life are acceptable. Fewer things in life are good. Only one thing in any aspect of life can be called BEST. What makes something the best? I like this acronym:

B = Blessing. A blessing produces good in an individual's life. A genuine blessing overflows from one person into the lives of others. A blessing that is good for one person becomes good for every other person in the equation, including one's enemies. A blessing produces. It generates activities and attitudes that are giving, loving, merciful, and kind. No blessing is intended to be hoarded or used for extreme self-indulgence. Every blessing is intended to be enjoyed and shared. Always remember, you are blessed to BE a blessing!

E = Excellence. The best is the highest quality possible, the supreme effort, the greatest value, and the closest to perfection that can be attained by human beings. No person is capable of getting life right all the time; certainly no man-made device can work with precision and beauty forever. But the BEST comes as close as possible to what is considered ideal or optimum as much of the time as possible, for as long as possible.

S = Satisfying. The best things satisfy the most. The BEST health, the BEST love, the BEST appreciation, and the BEST accomplishments are those that bring a sense of meaning, completion, or fulfillment to life. The best things of life do not just bring momentary happiness; they are grounded in deep inner joy.

T = Timelessness. The best things have an eternal element embedded in them. They produce benefits, results, and rewards that extend beyond one's lifetime.

Ultimately, the BEST things are positive, hope filled, and godly.

God's Plan Is Always BEST

I do not believe God is capable of creating evil. He certainly doesn't reward it or honor it. He moves against it at all times. His plans and purposes are for the GOOD of humankind, individually and collectively. He desires our utmost and highest. In the end, He wants us to make the choices that will ensure that we live with Him forever.

Many people dismiss God's goodness and God's good plan without ever really having a relationship with God or understanding His plan. I routinely encounter people who think that everything related to religion is expressed in negative terms.

I totally agree that the Bible provides the comprehensive, authoritative definition of what is BEST for all people in all ages and in all aspects of life. I am concerned, however, that a person who seeks to base his life on the Bible really knows what the Bible says.

Just when I think I've heard all of the errors pertaining to what is and isn't in the Bible, somebody will say something I haven't heard before! I heard a woman say not long ago, "Cleanliness is next to godliness."

"My mother sure believed that," I said, trying to establish a point of agreement.

She glared at me. "It isn't just your mother. It's what the Bible says."

Well . . . not really.

There are lots of folklore sentiments that are good, but they aren't in the Bible. The Bible doesn't say that we should eat an apple a day to keep the doctor away. It doesn't say that early birds get worms. It doesn't even say that those who go to bed early will be those who rise early and become healthy, wealthy, and wise.

I'm not declaring that these are bad truisms. I'm just saying they aren't biblical. And when it comes to determining what is BEST in life, my personal choice is to begin with God's Word and go from there. I heartily encourage you to read and study God's manual for the BEST in your life.

My foremost concern is that you recognize that blind spots often occur because we have not diligently sought out the BEST that might be possible for our lives. Many people have bought into lies and false teachings from their childhoods. They have never reexamined for themselves the cultural or family definitions that were given to them for good, better, and BEST.

Wisdom is the spirit of God that enables us to differentiate not only between good and evil but also between good and BEST, and empowers us to implement the will of God in any and every situation.

If I want what is BEST, I will look for the BEST in people, situations, and things. In the process of looking for the BEST, I will minimize the worst. Simultaneously, I will be dealing with my Blind Spots.

Instead of seeking out the best ways to apply what we know to be the best truth, we often opt for the applications, choices, and decisions that are easy. Or the thing that screams the loudest, demands the most, or has the squeakiest wheel.

We run from one crisis to the next and often run headlong into a blind spot. We find ourselves in a situation that spins out of our control until we collapse in exhaustion. Then we scrape ourselves up off the floor and say, "What happened?"

If you have never taken the time to consider the BEST life you can possibly live, I invite you to do that right now. Take a blank sheet of paper and list various aspects of your life to one side. Then next to each aspect, put down a few words, but not more than a sentence, that define what you imagine to be the BEST of you.

I recommend these categories, but you may think of others:

My BEST Life

Relationship with God:

Personal character traits:

Relationship with spouse:

Relationship with children:

Friendships:

Physical health:

Finances:

Material possessions:

Use of time:

Priorities in any given day:

Knowledge base (mental and intellectual health):

Work life:

Church life:

Spiritual disciplines:

Community:

Retirement:

Eternity:

Legacy:

Stress level:

Once you have a clear picture of what you consider to be BEST, ask yourself, "How can I get there?" Very few people are already living their best possible life. But most people have a starting point for what they might do to improve their current situation. Identify your best first step in each of the categories you listed.

When you have a clear understanding of BEST, you will recognize the best first steps for what they are. You will begin to see blind spots of mediocrity, waste, and loss. Problems will begin to have more solutions. Voids will begin to be filled with meaning and a sense of satisfaction. Dreams will begin to be fulfilled.

S Is for Surface

The question we must ask at the surface level of life is, what IS? And by this I mean, what REALLY is?

Most people live at a surface level. They take in only as much life as their senses can hold. What they see, smell, touch, hear, or taste tells them everything they choose to know about life. While I am not an advocate of living only at the surface level of life, I do understand that in order to stay alive, a person must live at a surface level at least some of the time. Those who live with their heads in the clouds usually stumble over boulders or fall off the edges of cliffs. It truly is possible for a person to be so heavenly minded that he is of no earthly good.

If we see life only at the surface, however, we'll miss many of the deeper and richer things of life. We'll also make thousands of errors. Even so, let's recognize at the outset of this discussion that the vast majority of people do not look deep into life. They evaluate life in a superficial way. We need to recognize that and have compassion for those who live this way, and make a concerted effort not to be like other people when it comes to living by default.

As an author, I have learned that half of all book-buying decisions are made on the basis of a person's appraisal of a book cover. We may know the phrase, don't judge a book by its cover, but that phrase is counter to what book-buying statistics tell us. My challenge to you is to always look beyond the cover of a book—and a person.

In our culture, people tend to buy on impulse. We are taken in by the point-of-purchase display at the sales counter. People tend to buy the products offered as samples at the supermarket on Saturday mornings, even if we have absolutely no idea how to grill buffalo so it tastes anything but gamy and tough.

At the surface level, every problem looks like a problem. Indeed, most of life looks like a series of problems. The surface of life is jumbled, random, confusing, and often, a sensory overload.

At the surface level, every action can seem appropriate, every idea beneficial, every emotion justified. To avoid these blind spots, we must become adept at a basic superficial skill. We must be able to differentiate between WHAT IS and WHAT APPEARS TO BE.

The challenge of seeing lies in seeing what truly IS, not just what appears to be or what you sense or feel might be a reality.

Have you ever walked into a room and had a slightly uneasy feeling, but you just couldn't seem to pinpoint what was bothering you? Don't discount that feeling. In all likelihood, there is something happening in that room that is directly related to your uneasy feeling. Ask questions until you discover what it is. Then, even if you discover what REALLY is, don't judge first. Learn first. The purpose for learning what is, is to learn and grow using what can help us with our own blind spots, not point out others' blind spots. Remember, your unique 1% can only be Discovered, Developed, and Deployed if you deal with your blind spots. Dealing with yours is . . . what REALLY is . . . important.

These four key questions are worthy of asking at all times and about every situation, relationship, or experience in our lives:

1. WHAT IS? (What really, truly IS and not just what appears or seems to be?)

2. WHAT WAS? (What has been in the past?)

3. WHAT IS BEST? (At this time, in this situation, with the people you are with, what's best?)

4. WHAT IS POSSIBLE? (With you involved, what can happen?)

If a person makes finding answers to these questions an ongoing quest, blind spots that should be addressed will be addressed. Blind spots that should be eliminated will be eliminated. Blind spots that should be filled in with positive, appropriate, and beneficial responses to one's self and one's life will be filled in.

The fact is that everybody has Blind Spots, but not everybody deals with them. It's easier to point out the blind spots in others than to discover our own, Develop a solution in ourselves, and Deploy our greatness by having dealt with the blind spots. The real value of dealing with your blind spots is that when you courageously do so, you elevate your 1%. You move beyond normalcy and mediocrity to a position of elevated strength. You position yourself to exponentially multiply your 1% Factor.

THINK, BE, DO

THINK: Discover

What paradigms are you Discovering that you may have that have caused particular blind spots?

Seek to Discover your blind spots. Make a commitment to Discover areas that risk hindering your 1% Factor.

BE: Develop

Develop a strategy for revealing and improving your blind spots.

Find people who love you for you, and ask them to be honest about the blind spots they see.

DO: Deploy

Deploy what you have become experienced in based on the unique experiences you have been through.

Deploy an ongoing strategy to deal with your blind spots.

Your 1% Genius

Everybody is a genius. But if you judge
a fish by its ability to climb a tree, it will
live its whole life believing that it is stupid.
—— ALBERT EINSTEIN

In 1952, on the island of Koshima, scientists began to study the Japanese monkey *Macaca fusucata*. They provided them with sweet potatoes that had been dropped in the sand. The monkeys liked the sweet potatoes, but they did not like the sand on the outside of them. An eighteen-month-old female named Imo learned that she could solve the problem by washing the potatoes in a nearby stream. She then showed her mother. By 1958, all the young monkeys had learned to wash the sand off of the sweet potatoes before they ate them. Only the adult monkeys who chose to learn from their children did. The other adult monkeys kept eating the dirty sweet potatoes.

Then it happened! In autumn of that same year, one monkey washed the dirt off of a sweet potato and in one day, the whole tribe began to do the same. The monkey who washed the sweet potato wasn't the leader of the tribe but was one that became known as the Hundredth Monkey. While the exact number of monkeys who learned to solve the dirt problem was unknown, the scientists determined that when this particular monkey learned the skill, it created the genius for others to follow suit. The most surprising discovery to the scientists was when this genius phenomenon happened to ONE monkey, and that empowered the whole tribe of monkeys to learn the skill of washing, it didn't stop on the island of Koshima! The hundredth-monkey effect created a problem-solving genius awareness with colonies of monkeys on other islands, who began washing their sweet potatoes as well.

Although the exact number may vary, the hundredth-monkey phenomenon means that when only a limited number of people are exposed to a problem-solving innovative strategy, it remains limited in influence. But there is a specific point when a unique person aligns with a new awareness, something almost super-natural happens so that this problem-solving awareness reaches everyone![1]

The world is waiting on your 1% Genius, which no one else has, to bring something super-natural to the world that the world has never seen! As you D-D-D Your 1%, your genius is being released to the world and, maybe just as significantly, you will help others to wash the dirt off their sweet potatoes.

What Is a Genius?

Thomas Edison said, "Genius is 1% inspiration and 99% perspiration."

F. Scott Fitzgerald said, "The test of a first-rate intelligence is the ability to hold two opposed ideas in the mind at the same time, and still retain the ability to function. Genius is the ability to put into effect what is on your mind."

Ralph Waldo Emerson said, "Speak what you think today in words as hard as cannon balls, and tomorrow speak what tomorrow thinks in hard words again, though it contradict everything you said today. . . . To be great is to be misunderstood. To believe your own thought, to believe that what is true for you in your private heart is true for all men—that is genius."

William James said, "Genius means little more than the faculty of perceiving in an unhabitual way."

Henry Van Dyke said, "Genius is talent set on fire by courage."

In Roman mythology, a Genius was a guardian spirit that protected an individual throughout her life. Every living person was endowed with a specific genius to whom yearly offerings were made, generally on the person's birthday. The accomplishments of an individual were often attributed to his genius. In addition to each individual's genius, there were geniuses who protected tribes, towns, places, and the Roman state. A particularly important genius was the Genius Populi Romani, guardian of Rome.[2]

1828 Webster's definition: *Genius* is "a peculiar nature, disposition, aptitude or character that directs one's course of life."

My definition: A Genius is someone who can solve a problem that others can't. She knows what to do, how to do it, when to do it, why she needs to do it, and, because she is willing to do it, she is a GENIUS!

What Makes a Genius a Genius?

For years, scholars and researchers have tried to explain genius by giving vital statistics, as if piles of data somehow illuminated genius. In his 1904 study of genius, Havelock Ellis noted that most geniuses are fathered by men older than thirty, had mothers younger than twenty-five, and were usually sickly as children. Scholars reported that many were celibate (Descartes), others were fatherless (Dickens), or motherless (Darwin). In the end, the piles of data illuminated nothing.[3]

Has anyone ever said to you, "You are a genius!" Have you ever said that to anyone else? In both cases, I bet it was said to you because you solved someone's problem. Or you said it because someone solved your problem. The bottom line is this: the better you are at solving problems, the more of a Genius you are!

Geniuses don't approach problems the same way everyone else does. Most people try to solve a problem by looking at what it is in the present and then going back to what has been in the past. Unfortunately, many people do not realize that their self-image is partially shaped by their conclusions about life in the past. We don't even realize the walls we have built that insulate our problem-solving Genius. We don't realize the Great Barrier Reefs that we have formed that limit our greatness. Albert Einstein said, "No problem can be solved from the same level of consciousness that created it."

So how can you think like a Genius? Is it possible? When it comes to problem solving, I want to suggest to you that it is easier than you would think. In fact, your 1% Genius is activated when you start focusing on the solution rather than the problem.

I Am Your Problem

I am a reality in your every day.

*I have many names, many faces, many shapes
and I come in every size and color.*

I am blamed for more failures than anything or anyone else.

*I am no respecter of persons. I do not play
favorites and I never choose sides.*

*Within me are invisible seeds of greatness and
immeasurable fields of frustration. What you choose to
do with me will make you better or make you bitter.*

*The people who don't want me the most,
inevitably have the most of me.*

*Without me there would be zero success! In fact, I am
the driving force behind all achievement, and the better
you get at dealing with me, the better you will be.*

*It's not a matter of IF you will face me, but WHEN
you will face me . . . and with that, let me make you
a guarantee: I will be in your face every day.*

*I am the one thing in your life that has the potential
to help you Think Bigger . . . Be Better . . . and Do
the Impossible in every area of your life.*

*The most important thing about me that you need to
know is that I am waiting every day to be used by you—
or, in worst case scenarios, to be used against you.*

Who am I?

*I am your Problem—and in case no one has
told you, my last name is Solution!*

Problem-Solving Genius

There are four core things that Geniuses do to become great
problem solvers:

1. Geniuses identify THE problem.

2. Geniuses A-A-P everything.

3. Geniuses define problems.

4. Geniuses benefit from the problem.

Geniuses Identify THE Problem

Early in the days of the space program, our astronauts and
engineers discovered that ink didn't flow at zero gravity. Writing
was an important part of documenting the exploration of space,
and leaky pens were a messy problem. One company set out to
solve it. A decade and twelve million dollars later, that company
produced a pen that writes upside down, on any surface (including crystal), under water, and in temperatures ranging from
below freezing to 300° Fahrenheit.

The Russians opted to use pencils.

The Russians had focused on the REAL problem—the need
for a reliable writing tool in space. We focused on what we
perceived to be OUR problem—our ink pens weren't working,
and we wanted ones that would.

There is usually a significant difference between the REAL
problem and what we perceive to be OUR problem.

There's another principle at work here as well: the solution to
a problem rarely lies in your current resources. New resources,
including new creative ideas, are likely to be required.

The reality is that the problem is never the problem, but the
way we see the problem. The solution to a problem, therefore,
always begins with our thinking.

Baby Genius Steps

To identify the problem like a genius does, ask more questions to bore into the cause.

Step #1: Locate the real problem. Consider this a thinking-alignment issue. Keep probing, asking questions, and discussing until you can identify the real problem and state it in a single sentence. For any solution to be effective, it needs to be in proper alignment with the foremost or central problem. Very often the real problem is the exact opposite of what a person thinks is the real problem at the outset.

Consider the husband and wife who argue frequently about the family budget. There just doesn't seem to be enough money to reach the end of the month. The husband contends that his wife has a spending problem. The wife contends that they have an earning problem (often stated that the husband has an earning problem). Both are partly right. But the *real* problem is a communication and budgeting problem—this couple hasn't agreed on how much will be spent on what on a month-to-month basis. They don't need bargains or raises as much as they need a budget—and more specifically, a budget they both help create and agree upon.

Step #2: Isolate the real problem. Problems tend to stick together like pieces of wet paper. Before long, conversations about problems can degenerate into "you always" and "you never" accusations. Very little gets resolved at that point.

To isolate the problem, a person must focus on the distinguishing characteristics of the *particular* problem. This can often be determined by asking a series of why questions. Let me take you through a couple lines of such questioning.

The problem appears to be that you are always late on the completion of assignments—perhaps not intentionally, and perhaps not in ways that impact an overall process, but consistently late nevertheless. Consider these questions:

Q: Why am I late in completing many projects? (surface, obvious problem)
A: I procrastinate in getting started.

Q: Why do I procrastinate? (motivational problem)
A: I don't like the project.

Q: Why don't I like the project? (preferences problem)
A: It seems unnecessary.

Q: Why do I think the project is unnecessary? (priorities problem)
A: Because my boss is inept.

Q: Why do I work for an inept boss? (relational problem)
A: Because of my own insecurities.

The reality is that most people procrastinate for reasons other than not liking a particular project. Four of the biggest reasons for procrastination I have observed are: low passion level, a lack of personal excellence, too many other competing projects and lack of leadership to prioritize them, and fear of failure—either that the project will not be completed to perfection, or that the project will not be completed to a level of satisfaction.

I want to encourage you to stir up your passion; commit to Thinking, Being, and Doing your best; learn to prioritize work; and confront fears of failure. Discover what motivates you, and then activate your own self-leadership.

The fact is, many people who are consistently late in completing projects do not put adequate focus on themselves. They

blame others for everything from lack of cooperation to unreasonable deadlines.

Consider another example of questioning. This one is related
to a perceived problem of starting things that never get done.

Q: Why do I have so many things in process, with so few
   projects completed?
A: I am not focused in my work. (In other words, I try to do
   too many things simultaneously.)

Q: Why can't I stay focused?
A: Because I allow myself to be interrupted or distracted.

Q: Why do I allow interruptions and distractions?
A: Because I don't want to disappoint or be rude to people who
   are interrupting me or distracting me.

Q: Why do I struggle with this?
A: I have never been good at setting personal boundaries,
   because I don't want to be rejected.

Aha! Learn to set boundaries and you are likely to accomplish
things important to you.

A man once said to me during a coaching session, "I struggle
with criticism. I just can't seem to take criticism from others
without getting angry or defensive. I don't really like to argue,
but I seem to argue frequently with those who are critical of me."
My response: "Why do you think you struggle with criticism?"

I hadn't really meant to open a psychological can of worms,
but once the can was opened, I chose to listen to this man's
defining moment of an early childhood that was filled with
criticism and very little affirmation. His defining moments had
not produced the momentum to become miraculous moments in

his life. My response was to encourage him and advise him to seek professional counseling so he might live a happier life and be more successful in his relationships with his wife and two children.

The key point here is that most REAL problems end up being highly personal problems. They reside in the way we think, the way we believe, the attitudes we hold, and in a more generalized way, the patterns of thinking that give rise to patterns of speaking and behaving.

In the vast majority of cases, the REAL problem is not objective or outside one's own self. It lies within. It isn't a matter of leaky ink pens, but a matter of personal areas of pain that have never been fully healed.

People have basic needs that must be met or else they result in all sorts of behavioral problems. Solely because you are a human being, you have a built-in need for:

- Affirmation: in the form of appreciation, recognition, and encouragement

- Affection: in the form of positive touching and words of love

- Value: in the form of successful use of your talents employed toward ends that you believe are honorable

If you don't have enough of any of the above, you will react to life in negative ways; perhaps small and subtle ways but nevertheless negative ways. You may not be aware that this is happening. You may not think you have ANY unmet needs. Or you may not have much skill in seeking out positive, healthful ways of getting your needs met.

Those are challenges you need to face head-on. The real source of a problem lies at the core of your own spiritual and psychological self.

Step #3: Amalgamate. There comes a point when identifying and isolating need to result in a game plan. *To amalgamate* is "to unite" or "to mix and synergize to make a uniform compound." In this case, we want to make a uniform plan of action.

Consider again the couple having financial problems. After a calm and objective discussion of their problem, they may have isolated various surface issues: not enough income, no budget, too much unnecessary spending, and even bad advice about good money management. They may have also been able to discuss underlying issues by asking:

- Why do we feel we need certain things?

- Why do we think we deserve a lifestyle we can't yet afford?

- Whom are we trying to impress?

- What does owning stuff do for us?

- What empowerment do we each feel in buying and spending, or in saving and investing?

Confront your blind spots as an individual and as a couple. The bottom line is often not pretty. Words such as *greed, poor self-worth, pride,* and *envy* tend to pop up. But none of these are terminal conditions, and all can be addressed and changed.

The amazing thing about the amalgamation process is this: you will often find that as you drill down to the core problem related to several surface problems, you hit the same real problem in other areas of your life. The same core problem shows up again and again. Deep issues tend to manifest themselves at the surface of life in a variety of ways.

I know a man who has difficulty prioritizing. All things seem of equal weight or value to him. You can imagine how the lack of priority impacts his ability to get projects completed at work. The problem also impacts his relationship with his wife and children. He simply lacks the ability to manage either time or resources. The problem pops up again and again; it's the same problem, just repackaged.

It will be vital for this man to amalgamate if he is going to make progress. He must get to the core problem and then see the many ways this problem manifests if he is going to make significant and lasting changes that extend to the whole of his life.

Amalgamation gives entrée to synergy, which is the concept that two or more things, people, or organizations working together produce a result that is greater than the normal sum of individual effects or capabilities. In other words, two plus two doesn't always equal four. It can be exponentially multiplied! Two working together on the same page toward the same goals can produce far more than the two individuals working separately could.

Amalgamation can also lead to negative synergy, or to the compounding of problems. Or it can lead to positive synergy resulting in multiple surface problems being resolved when a core problem is resolved.

It's Almalgamazing when we see synergy at work all around us. When people align themselves with other people who will HELP them and receive their help in return, great progress can be made!

Core problems lead to many surface problems. Core solutions can also lead to many surface solutions!

Step #4: Extrapolate. *To extrapolate* means "to draw conclusions about the future by making projections based on the past."

Imagine a graph that charts sales on a month-to-month basis. If the overall trend is upward, even though one month may be down a bit, then one can extrapolate an observation to conclude that sales are going up. Future inventories and activities can be planned based upon that extrapolation.

This principle works in every area of life. If you are able to see where things are headed, you can change course! If things are headed downward, start exploring what you might do to turn things around. If things are headed upward, explore options for increasing the upward momentum.

No trend line is automatic. But equally true—all trends can be impacted by intentional decisions.

> *To get a future focus, you need to look PAST your past!*

Don't get bogged down in what WAS. Turn your focus to what might be.

> *What has been is your past. What is, is your present. What is possible is your future. Never allow what has been or what is to keep you from what is possible. Your future is possible!*

Geniuses A-A-P Everything

In the midst of every problem, a process exists for solving the problem. I use a strategic process for Assessing, Addressing, and Progressing through situations to find optimal solutions and preventions to future problematic situations.

Stage #1: Assess. Assessing a problem or situation is the WHY and WHERE part of the equation. Before a problem or situation can be resolved, it is best to know WHY it occurred in the first place and WHERE you are in the process now. The best solution is preventing a future recurrence and putting parameters in place to eliminate any possibility of recurrence.

Stage #2: Address. Addressing is the WHAT question of the problem or situation. In addressing the WHAT, you will DEVELOP as many options to resolving the problem, finding a solution, and preventing future reoccurrence as you can imagine. No potential solution should be considered too large, too small, too bizarre, or too obscure. Do your own brainstorming, or invite a trusted colleague or family member to brainstorm with you. Throw as many things onto a blank piece of paper or whiteboard as possible. Don't limit yourself!

Most problems weren't created overnight, and finding the best solution may take more than a few minutes. Review the WHAT options you have listed. Explore them. Define them. DEVELOP the better ones to find the BEST one. The BEST is always the goal.

I have told my children for years, "Never allow the good to be the robber of the BEST." The BEST solution will have these characteristics:

- It will be the best for you and for everybody else involved.

- It will be a solution that makes maximum use of your talents and abilities.

- It will be a solution that excites you by its potential and motivates you to WANT to pursue it.

- It will be a realistic solution within acceptable risk boundaries.

- It will be a solution that causes no harm to you or others—physically, emotionally, or spiritually. The solution may require expenditure of funds or material resources. It may take time. But the application of funds, material resources, and time will be an INVESTMENT toward a realistic goal, with minimal risk of total loss.

- It will be a solution to proactively guard against future reoccurrence.

Stage #3: Progress. Progressing is the HOW question of the equation. It establishes the principles of DEPLOY—how to get where you want to be.

---

*There is no Great Progress
without Great Process.*

No problem is ever resolved in theory, except math problems on blackboards. Eventually, real-world problems are resolved by real-world ACTION. The place where people err is thinking they have resolved a problem if they have admitted it, talked about it, or made a one-time effort at a solution.

Admitting the problem is essential, but it solves nothing. Talking about the problem is helpful, and certainly having good discussions about the problem with a close family member or colleague can result in better understanding, a closer relationship, and perhaps even the freeing power of forgiveness. But talk can seem cheap if conversations do not produce lasting changes in behavior.

Consider the wife who works all day only to come home to a long list of household chores. She resents having to pick up her husband's dirty clothes that are lying on the bathroom floor. She resents having to take out the trash, mow the lawn, and make sure the car is washed. These are jobs she never saw her mother do. In her mind, these are husband chores. She complains. Then she tries the silent and distant treatment. Nothing works. Finally she says to her husband, "I've had it. We need to talk." He agrees, probably oblivious as to what she is upset about.

She describes her frustrations. He assures her that he loves her and that he means no harm. He didn't even know that she wanted him to do these chores. He asks her specifically what she wants him to do and she says, "Put your dirty clothes in the laundry basket. Take out the trash. Mow the lawn. Wash the car."

He says he will. But he doesn't. The wife comes again. "This is a problem!" He counters, "But you didn't say WHEN you wanted those things done." It never dawned on him that she would want it done before he watched his favorite sports event on TV.

The problem is not one of failing to admit the problem, identify it—at least on a surface level—or communicate about it. The problem remains unresolved if there's no ACTION. And furthermore, this principle kicks in: a problem will GROW if it is defined and communicated about but then nothing happens.

Each discussion about these household chores is going to grow more heated, and result in greater damage to the relationship, as time passes. For there to be REAL progress in solving the problem, there must be REAL effort that is visible and tangible in the REAL world.

The REAL problem is not the dirty clothes on the floor, the trash, the yard, or even the dirty car. The REAL problem is the husband not respecting his wife; he's treating her like his housekeeper and servant. He's not owning up to be a responsible, disciplined individual. He has no self-leadership! The REAL problem is a Self-Leadership issue, and one that he must resolve at HIS CORE LEVEL!

The A-A-P Triad will guide you to HAVE the solution to the problem, the situation resolved, and the parameters in place to prevent future reoccurrence because you took the steps required to Assess the problem completely, Address all possible solutions, and Progress the best solution to a final result.

But what about the solutions to problems that are more psychological or emotional in nature? Even these problems must have a solution that is tangible and real.

The A-A-P process can be used in all situations to Discover, Develop, and Deploy the BEST solution to resolve and eliminate future reoccurrences.

Geniuses Define Problems

I discussed this issue in Chapter 1, "Your Defining Moments," but there is an aspect worth repeating here. The tendency of people with long-standing problems is to make the problem the focal point of their entire life. All other issues, plans, dreams, or activities seem to orbit around the problem. So do conversations and relationships. The problem becomes paramount in its centrality. And the result is not only that the person is incapable of thinking about too many other things, but also every other person in the problem-focused person's work life, family life, church life, and community life eventually knows about the problem and its all-consuming hold on the problem-laden person's life.

I once knew a man—I'll call him Sam—who finally admitted his alcoholism. He had gone on drinking sprees from the time he was a teenager. Everybody knew Sam had a drinking problem. And when things got worse and Sam finally owned up to the problem, he was admitted to a detoxification center, and everyone knew about it. After his release from the hospital, he was intent on living a sober life. He told people openly that he was a recovering alcoholic. He told them . . . and told them . . . and told them. He scolded his friends who had once been his drinking buddies. He alienated each of them without offering any assistance. He railed against places that sold alcohol, to no effect. The truth was, Sam was as preoccupied with the IDEA of drinking as much or more so after treatment as he had been before.

I asked him on one occasion, "Sam, do you know why you started drinking in the first place?"

He said he was just a teenager. It made him feel like an adult. I wanted to know how he felt when he drank. He said he felt courageous and that nothing scared him. He said he was more outgoing and had more fun when he was drinking.

I asked if he felt like the center of attention. The response was yes and that he was a fun guy when he drank. But when he wasn't drinking, he was lifeless, dull, and not fun to be with.

I was surprised that the therapists at the detox center hadn't drilled down to this level. Sam was still seeking to be the center of attention. He still had a need for others to see him as a valuable and fun person when he didn't really see himself that way. He was using his NOT drinking in many of the same ways he had used his over-drinking.

The root problem in Sam's life was still the root problem. And in making sobriety the center of his entire life, he was forcing those closest to him to orbit around his inner problems rather than seeing how this one area of problem was just that—ONE AREA of problem.

In Chapter 7 I introduced the five Cs. Consider these five areas of life that are impacted by any serious problem:

1. **Character.** A problem—in believing, thinking, speaking, or behaving—will eventually impact your character. Be aware of that. For example, do you have a problem with criticism? Do you find that you recoil or overreact to those who criticize you? The problem will impact your ability to love others. You MUST learn to accept the ideas that are beneficial and throw out the rest of the critical commentary that comes your way. If you can't make this distinction and bifurcate the problem—separate or split it into two distinct parts—you will be plagued by the problem in ways that will eventually make YOU more critical, less joyful, less at peace, less generous, less loving, and a whole lot less fulfilled in life.

2. **Chemistry.** An abiding problem eventually pollutes the atmosphere around you. The more you wallow in your problem, the more you create an emotionally toxic dump site that others will avoid.

3. **Communication.** A problem that you allow to invade and overtake your life will enter into every conversation you have. Not long ago, I heard about a woman whose husband had divorced her. She was reeling in pain, bitterness, and anger. She blamed him for everything bad that was happening to her. And then I discovered that her "husband" that she considered to be at the core of all her life's problems had divorced her twenty-eight years ago! She had been married two times since then. Everybody this woman met, from clerks in department stores to people she sat next to on airplanes, heard about her tragic tale. If you don't progress beyond the problem, you'll find that you will never really have friends with whom you can have mutually meaningful conversations.

4. **Consistency.** Problems disrupt the routines of our lives. This is true for natural disasters and also true for emotional earthquakes, flood tides of sorrow, whirlwinds of anger, and sudden sinkholes of depression and despair. Problems can keep you from engaging in a consistency of excellence that produces reward in your life. In other words, your preoccupation with a problem can result in failure—even if you have good skills, good education, good training, and a good work history.

5. **Competency.** Problems can keep you from doing your best or growing into your best. They will hold you back from developing either the profession-related or interpersonal skills that result in recognition, appreciation, and reward.

If an unresolved problem can impact a person's life in these five Cs, let me flip that around so you can ask yourself vital questions in each area.

1. Is your overall **Character** more important than your immediate problem? If so, then how might you begin to solve your problem in ways that will BUILD and purify your character rather than tear it down? What areas of your character might you seek to develop and enhance as a direct means of addressing and overcoming your problem?

2. What kind of **Chemistry** do you have with people? What is the atmosphere you are creating around you? Are people drawn to you or driven away from you? Do people seem to shut down when you bring up certain issues or problems? Do people have a good time in your presence; do they seek you out, enjoy laughing with you, and say they miss you if they don't see you for a while?

3. What do you **Communicate** about? How often do you rehearse your problems? Why do you feel compelled to have everyone know your problem?

4. How **Consistent** are you? What are you proficient at doing? Is a problem impacting the quality or quantity of your work?

5. Are you developing greater and greater **Competency** in skills? Are you learning new things and applying that new information to the whole of your life?

Geniuses Benefit from the Problem

You may not be able to make all problems disappear from your life. You may not even be able to make a major problem in your life disappear completely. But you can choose to benefit from and grow because of your problem. When you choose to benefit from your problem, you are operating in Your 1% Genius!

Problems Are Fertilizer

A man I know once said, "I see problems as fertilizer. They aren't the soil of my life. But when mixed into the soil of my life, they can help good seeds of solution grow."

Choose to see the problem as an opportunity or a challenge from which you can learn something valuable or develop a character trait to a point of strength and resiliency. You can not only determine your personal perspective on a problem, but you can also choose whom you will follow and from whom you will learn. This is Genius!

Do not follow anybody down a problem road. If you see a person headed for disaster, refuse to go there with him. You may think you are walking alongside the person to help him, but if he refuses to listen to your good counsel, refuses to receive your encouraging words, or refuses to heed your warnings, make your final statement and walk away.

What helps the person with the bad or questionable character the most? They are able to observe a person with good character as she accomplishes goals, has fun, and loves other people. Your 1% Genius is a Transformational Way for others to follow. One of my favorite Genius verses is found in Proverbs 10:17 (AMP):

> He who heeds instruction and correction is (not
> only himself) in the way of life (but also) is a way
> of life for others. And he who neglects or refuses
> reproof (not only himself) goes astray (but also)
> causes to err and is a path toward ruin for others.

What does this profound verse tell us? When you get instruction and receive correction, you get divine direction for your life. But not only that, as your 1% Genius is developed by displaying what you have received, your 1% Genius Transformation also becomes a path for others to follow. You become the Hundredth Monkey!

Let's face it. Problems aren't going away. Everybody has problems. If you don't have one now, you will have one, sooner or later.

Most people run from their problems or try to ignore them in hopes they will go away. They won't. Other people will try to diminish the severity of their problems in hopes that things will get better without intervention. As a result, problems persist.

Very few people run toward their problems with the full intent of solving them. Your 1% Genius is activated every time you run toward the problem and don't back down! Every problem is practice for your next level. In fact, if you don't learn to solve the problems on the level you are on in life right now, you will never get to go to Your Next Level. How do you ultimately benefit from a problem? Every problem you solve shouts: "YOU WERE BORN TO SOLVE SOMEBODY'S PROBLEM! YOU ARE NOT A PROBLEM—YOU ARE THE SOLUTION TO ANY PROBLEM!"

Always remember this: if you never had any problems to solve, you would never know how much of a Genius YOU are!

Look at your hand right now. Look at the end of your fingers! Fingerprints nobody else has ever had—to solve problems that only your 1% Genius can solve! Go be UNSTOPPABLE today! Be somebody's solution! Walk into a room and say, "Don't worry! The SOLUTION just arrived!"

THINK, BE, DO

THINK: Discover

What is a Genius?

What makes a Genius a Genius?

What do you know you are good at? That is what makes you THE Solution!

BE: Develop

Develop your A-A-P skills. Assess what has been. Address what is. Progress what is possible!

DO: Deploy

Deploy your five Cs.

Be ready to solve any problem by activating your 1% Genius.

Your 1% Power

You are deploying the Power of Your 1% when your Think (how you think), Be (who you choose to be), Do (your attitude, behavior, and actions) makes those around you better.

My heart's desire in writing this book is to help you Discover, Develop, and Deploy Your 1%. Your 1% is Your Unstoppable Force! Your 1% is not just about you being different than everyone else. It is what empowers you to be the best YOU you can be!

Discovering Your Unstoppable Force

I am very grateful for my parents, who exposed me to the house of God early in life. They provided an opportunity for me to Discover God. I think this is one of the greatest things parents can do for their children. My parents never forced God on me. In fact, I would describe our family as nonreligious. We went to church not out of duty or because that was what our religion required. We went to connect with a loving God. Why would I mention this? Because I think there are many people who never Discover God because their previous religious experiences or their perceptions of God based on preconceptions about religion are holding them back.

Religion vs. Relationship with God

Why is it important that we differentiate between Religion and Relationship with God? Because God wants to have a relationship with YOU! What are some of the distinctive differences between Religion and Relationship with God?

- Religion is man-made. Relationship with God is God-given.

- Religion is man's search for God. Relationship with God is a discovery that God wants you to know Him.

- Religion is about trying to be good. Relationship with God is about trusting that God is good and He wants the best for you.

- Religion is about laws. Relationship with God is about love.

- Religion is about doing. Relationship with God is about being.

- Religion is about climbing a ladder to meet God. Relationship with God is about God lowering a ladder and sending Jesus to meet YOU.

- Religion is about rules and regulations. Relationship with God is about mercy and forgiveness.

A relationship with God is what God wants with you and for you. This has been the secret of my own D-D-D of my 1%! Don't rule out going to church. Rule out religion. Find a church where you can connect with God. If you go to one and you are bored, go somewhere else. If you grew up in a church and it was irrelevant to your life, just know there are great houses of God all over the world where you can connect with God. This is so important to you Discovering, Developing, and Deploying Your 1%. Give church another try, or give it a try for the first time. Give God a chance to prove His God-ness in your life.

Your 1% Power Comes from God

My parents weren't perfect by any means, but if there is one thing they did right, it was get me to church and give me a chance to connect with God. I believe that to realize your full potential of your 1%, you must open up your heart to a relationship with God. The Bible says in John 3:16–18 (MSG):

> This is how much God loved the world: He gave his Son,
> his one and only Son. And this is why: so that no one
> need be destroyed; by believing in him, anyone can have
> a whole and lasting life. God didn't go to all the trouble
> of sending his Son merely to point an accusing finger,
> telling the world how bad it was. He came to help, to
> put the world right again. Anyone who trusts in him
> is acquitted; anyone who refuses to trust him has long
> since been under the death sentence without knowing it.
> And why? Because of that person's failure to believe in
> the one-of-a-kind Son of God when introduced to him.

This has some powerful messages for your 1%:

- Your 1% Power to be loved and to love comes from God.

- Your 1% Power to be forgiven and to forgive comes from God.

- Your 1% Power to be blessed and to be a blessing comes from God.

- Your 1% Power to receive a miracle and to become a miracle for others comes from God.

Jesus prayed prayers in John 17:20–23 (NLT) that I believe are the revelation of Your Unstoppable Force—Your 1%!

> I am praying not only for these disciples but also for all who will ever believe in me through their message. I pray that they will all be one, just as you and I are one—as you are in me, Father, and I am in you. And may they be in us so that the world will believe you sent me.

> I have given them the glory you gave me, so they may be one as we are one. I am in them and you are in me. May they experience such perfect unity that the world will know that you sent me and that you love them as much as you love me.

You Have Been Given the Glory of God

Do you see it? Jesus is saying that He is giving US the same thing that God gave Him: the Glory of God! You, my friend, have been given the Glory of God. So could it be that the 1% differ-

ence between you and everyone else who has been born and will
be born is THE GLORY OF GOD?

I believe that each one of us has been given a deposit of
God's GLORY that nobody else has, to bring a unique dimen-
sion and expression of God to the earth that nobody else can
bring! I have had the privilege of traveling all over the world,
and whether I am in London, Paris, Israel, Greece, or one of
the many other countries I have traveled, I have never seen
two people who are exactly alike. Twins are the closest thing in
the world. They are one gene split and, as I mentioned before,
they can look alike, talk alike, and sound alike, but each has a
unique fingerprint.

Why would God do this? Why would He make people so
distinctive in their appearances and yet make 99% of all human
DNA the same? There is only a 1% difference between every
human that has ever been born or will be born. And yet, it is a
very distinctive difference indeed!

My hope for you is that you will Discover not only how much
God loves YOU, but you will also discover that you have been
given the Glory of God that I believe is your 1% that makes YOU
an Unstoppable Force!

Developing Your Unstoppable Force

How do you become an Unstoppable Force? How can you be
Unstoppable in your marriage, in your business, in your
finances, in your relationships, in your life?

You Have to Know WHO Jesus Is

In Matthew 16:13–19 (NLT) of the Bible, Jesus addresses the
question of the ages:

When Jesus came to the region of Caesarea Philippi, he
asked his disciples, "Who do people say that the Son of
Man is?" "Well," they replied, "some say John the Baptist,
some say Elijah, and others say Jeremiah or one of the
other prophets." Then he asked them, "Who do you say I
am?" Simon Peter answered, "You are the Messiah, the
Son of the living God." Jesus replied, "You are blessed,
Simon son of John, because my Father in heaven has
revealed this to you. You did not learn this from any
human being. Now I say to you that you are Peter [which
means "rock"], and upon this rock I will build my church,
and all the powers of hell will not conquer it. And I will
give you the keys of the Kingdom of Heaven. Whatever you
forbid on earth will be forbidden in heaven, and whatever
you permit on earth will be permitted in heaven."

For Your 1% Power to be fully functional, you need to answer
the question Jesus asks of His own disciples, "Who do you say
that I am?" If you will open your heart up to God, read the Bible,
and ask God to speak to you, I believe He will. If you will declare
that Jesus is the only Son of God and ask Him to come into your
heart, he will forgive your sins—those things in your life that
keep you from reaching your full God-given potential. He will
bless you and give you the "keys of the kingdom" that whatever
you forbid or permit on earth will happen from heaven! Now
that's POWERFUL!

You Have to Know Who YOU Are

Who are you? What makes you different? Your FINGERPRINT!
We have discussed this fact throughout this book. The only
thing humankind has known to do with a fingerprint, until
recent years, is to use it to identify someone at the scene of a

crime. In other words, the only time a fingerprint was important to anybody was if someone needed to be identified because of a criminal act.

If you will believe, like I do, that it was God who gave you the unique fingerprint that you have and that is something great that God has done for you; if you will believe that you have been given the Glory of God as Jesus said; if you will believe that there is something so special about you that nobody else has; if you will believe that you have a deposit of God's Glory in you . . . then, you can begin to develop your 1%—the Glory of God deposited in you by Jesus. You can begin to know who you are because you know who He IS! When you acknowledge Jesus Christ as your Savior and Lord of Your life, and you life sentence Him as such, the Glory of God is revealed in you and through you. He begins to bless the works of your hands so that everywhere you go, your fingerprints leave an indelible imprint. You begin to bring your 1% Power to every person, in every situation, everywhere you go!

In Chapter 5, I shared about my dad and how God revealed to me that I could love him in a way he had never been loved by his father. It was my operating in my 1%. I remember him taking me to Muskogee, Oklahoma, to meet his dad, whom he barely knew. I was twelve years old, and I remember pulling into the poorest neighborhood I had ever seen at that time. We walked through the overgrown grass to the front door of the house that was only a screen door with many holes. My dad's dad told us to come in.

I stepped into a dirt-floor house with dilapidated furniture and filth. I had never seen anything like it. It wasn't about impoverished conditions as much as it was about a poverty mentality. My father exchanged a few words with his dad, and we left. As we were walking back to the car, I said, "I never want to come here again." My dad said, "That is why I brought you. I wanted you to know this is what I came from, but this is not who WE are."

I am convinced that you can know fully who you are and develop your 1% to your full God-given potential if you know WHO Jesus is.

Know What You Were Put on the Earth to Do

When I think about Mamaw, I am so grateful that she knew what she was put on the earth to do. Her 1% was characterized by the way she lived her life On Purpose every day. The following are just a few ways that she operated in her 1% Power. I call them:

Mamaw's Tenets for Life

1. You cannot dictate everything that happens to you, but you can dictate what happens in you.

2. Because you can dictate what happens in you, you can determine your outward response.

3. You cannot control what other people do to you, but you can control what you do to other people.

4. You are not responsible for the actions of others, but you are responsible for your own actions.

5. When you choose to Be the Best You Can Be, you will See the Best in others.

6. Never speak a negative word about anybody.

7. Never, never, never, never, never, never, never give up!

8. That which does not kill you strengthens you.

9. Pray for everyone, about everything, all the time.

10. God is faithful.

11. God is in control.

12. Wash your hands before every meal.

13. Brush your teeth after every meal.

14. Hope against hope.

15. Believe against belief.

16. Do not waiver in your faith in God.

17. Consider others before yourself.

18. Give thanks to God for everything, even for things you may not welcome in your life.

Deploying Your Unstoppable Force

What does *Deploy* mean? "To put, do, create, or move something to a useful place." It is one thing to Discover Your 1%. It is another to Develop Your 1%. But the most important thing you can do in your life is Deploy Your 1% Power! Take these approaches:

- Deploy Your Think, Be, Do: Think beyond your normal self every day, and your Vision will grow stronger, your Mission will be accomplished, and your Purpose will come to pass. Decide what it is in life that you want to Have and align Your Think, Be, Do to make it possible.

- Deploy Your Leadership: As you lead yourself every day to do what needs to be done, when it needs to be done, you will become empowered to lead others. When you understand the difference between Normalship and Leadership, you become a Change Agent for anything you want to change.

- Deploy Your Life Sentences: Begin to speak the life sentences over your life that sentence your life to seize opportunities and succeed. No one talks more to you than YOU! So learn to speak the right things to yourself that produce the results that you want. A great life sentence every day is: "I can do all things through Christ who strengthens me," from Philippians 4:13 (NKJV).

- Deploy Your Winning Edge: Practice being a Winner. Joe Montana shared a story with me that every time Jerry Rice caught a football in practice, he ran it for a touchdown. No matter where he was on the practice field, he would run all the way to the end zone. The whole practice had to wait on Jerry running the length of the field after every catch, in every practice. It is no accident that Jerry Rice holds the NFL record for most touchdowns in a career!

You've Got the Power!

My father and his colleagues in the fingerprinting division of a police force used fingerprints to identify criminals and deviants. Today, criminologists use the 1% difference in our DNA to identify criminals as well as to exonerate those who are falsely accused. Why use these methods? Because DNA and fingerprints are unique—and consistently reliable.

Year in and year out, your fingerprints remain the same. You have the same fingerprints now that you had when you were five years old, and they will be the fingerprints you have if you live to be 150. No matter how many times the skin cells on your hand reproduce, your fingerprint will remain the same. The same is true for your DNA. Your identification remains the same from conception to death.

Even against the background of so many things you cannot change, and so many things that are unchanging identification factors, you CAN change how you think, how you feel, how you relate to others, and how you relate to God to a great degree. You cannot press beyond the boundaries of your gifts or your personality, but you can make vital choices about how you activate your will to make decisions that frame your character and your behavior.

Living Your 1%

You can be great in every area of your life. You can live a life of excellence. You can develop your 1% Power with all that your greatness entails. Every person can experience their greatness, share their greatness, and elevate their greatness by D-D-Ding their 1%. It's a choice that brings fulfillment, meaning, and purpose.

Your 1% Power is not intended to be displayed only once. This is not destination; it's a journey! Your 1% Power is intended to be expressed in your thinking—all the time. Your 1% Power is to be expressed by your character—all the time. Your 1% Power is to be expressed in your behavior—all the time. It is who you are and who God made you to be.

Remember, Your 1% has the power it has for one simple reason—God!

Look at Your Hand

Look at your life as your fingerprint. God gave you a unique fingerprint. Look at your DNA. God gave you unique DNA that no one else has! Look at your eyes. God gave you an iris no one else shares. YOU are truly unique! That means you have greatness in you that no one else has because God put His glory in you unlike anyone else on earth!

To realize your 1% Factor is to realize that God is your creator. He wants to be your Lord and Savior. God gave you His Son, Jesus Christ, who was judged on our behalf that we might have all power and everlasting life.

God Looks at Your Heart

God created you, gave you dominion, and empowered you with uniqueness like no other person on earth. He gave you His Son as a sacrifice, offers you everlasting life, and provides you the strength you need to accomplish anything and everything.

My question to you today is, will you accept Jesus Christ as your Lord and Savior today so you can experience the Glory of God in your life? It's your choice. If so, it would be my greatest joy to pray a prayer with you. Repeat out loud after me:

Dear Heavenly Father, I ask you to forgive me where I have missed the mark. I choose today to accept Jesus Christ as my Lord and Savior. Thank you, Father, for my uniqueness. Empower me today, Lord, to Discover my 1% so that I can live a purposeful life. Help me today to live every day with your power in my life. Thank you, Lord. Amen.

THINK, BE, DO

THINK: Discover

Discover Your 1% Power.

BE: Develop

Develop your relationship with God.

DO: Deploy

Deploy your greatness to the world!

Acknowledgments

I am eternally grateful to my Mamaw, Bessie G. Ferguson. I want to both dedicate this book to her and acknowledge her immeasurable influence in my life. She was the most wonderful woman I have ever known. She is my hero. This book would never have been written if she had not prayed me back to life. Her courage and faith to believe for my miracle and the miraculous outcome were documented on the front page of the *Dallas Morning News*.

When I started Elevate Life Church, on January 9, 2000, she was very sick and could not attend. I drove to my parents' house in east Texas where she was living and we watched a videotape of our first service. We laughed and cried together. That was January 11. The next morning, one day before her eighty-eighth birthday, she went to be with Jesus.

The last thing my Mamaw did on earth was to watch the first church service of a church her grandson founded, who she had prayed back to life. I thank God for the privilege He gave me to share some of her heavenly reward on earth before she went to heaven. Most of all, I thank God for a woman who lived her 1% every day and became a transformational example of a life well lived.

I love you Mamaw . . .

I wish to acknowledge Jeff Brewer as a Mighty Man in my life. Thank you for your passion, energy, encouragement, and effort to get my 1% in print. Thank you for all your work and belief in me.

I wish to acknowledge Tad Tomaseski, who has been my friend, co-laborer, for over twenty-four years. Thank you for being a living epistle of the 1% message and making me believe that this life message really does work. Thank you for standing with me and believing in me for all these years.

To my best friend, Scott Unclebach . . . thank you for being the primary anvil that I have beat my leadership out on. Your love for me has helped to shape me into the man and leader I am.

I would like to thank my editor, Nancy Hancock, at Harper-One for her professional sweetness and helping to make my first book a joyful experience. Thank you for making me better through this process.

For my Acknowledgement Exclamation, I want to thank my high school girlfriend, my college fiancée, my forever lover, my teacher, my everyday anvil, my consummate confidante, my endless encourager, and lover of my soul, the mother of the three most amazing children, and the greatest person I know . . . my wife, Sheila.

About the Author

Keith Craft is the founder and lead pastor of the mega church Elevate Life Church in Frisco, Texas (7,000 congregants). He speaks in the world's largest business/success seminars and has shared the stage with former world leaders such as Bill Clinton, George Bush, Mikhail Gorbachev, and Margaret Thatcher. For the past twenty years he has spoken alongside Super Bowl winning coaches such as Mike Ditka, Don Shula, Mike Shanahan, and Tony Dungy; MVP quarterbacks such as Terry Bradshaw, Joe Montana, and Peyton Manning; and entertainers such as Jerry Lewis, Bill Cosby, and Goldie Hawn. As a leadership coach and strategist, Keith is also the founder of Leadershipology.com, an online quote service.

Notes

CHAPTER 2: YOUR X FACTOR FOR SUCCESS

1. Robynne Boyd, "Do People Only Use 10 Percent of Their Brains?" *Scientific American,* February 7, 2008, http://www.scientificamerican.com/article.cfm?id=people-only-use-10-percent-of-brain.

2. Russell Conwell, *Acres of Diamonds* (Minneapolis: Filiquarian Publishing, 2007).

CHAPTER 6: YOUR LEADERSHIP

1. United States Department of Labor, "Occupational Employment and Wages," May 2012.

CHAPTER 7: TOUR T-N-T

1. Catalina Woldarsky Meneses and Leslie S. Greenberg, "Interpersonal Forgiveness in Emotion-Focused Couples' Therapy Relating Process to Outcome," *Journal of Marital and Family Therapy,* September 8, 2012.

CHAPTER 11: YOUR 1% GENIUS

1. Patrick K. Porter, *Awaken the Genius: Mind Technology for the 21st Century* (Dallas: Pure Light Publications, 1994).

2. Grolier Electronic Publications, *The New Grolier Multimedia Encyclopedia* (New York: Grolier Electronic Publications, 1994).

3. Michael Michalko, "How Geniuses Think," The Creativity Post, April 28, 2012.

6/15 - WS
12115 B
6116 O
12116 H
6117 W